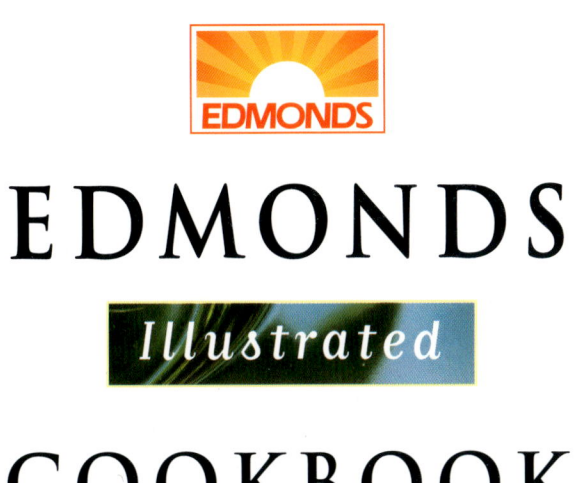

EDMONDS
Illustrated
COOKBOOK

EDMONDS

Illustrated

COOKBOOK

Hodder Moa Beckett

CONTENTS

INTRODUCTION 6

BAKING 10
*Breads & Buns 12   Muffins, Loaves, Scones 18
Cakes 24   Biscuits 44   Slices 54*

LIGHT MEALS 64
Nibbles 66   Breakfasts 72   Light Meals 76

HOME-COOKED MEALS 84
*Pasta 86   Seafood 94   Meat 106
Chicken 116   Vegetables 124*

DESSERTS 130
Cold Desserts 132   Hot Puddings 146

PRESERVES 156
Icings, Custard, Pastries, Dressings & Sauces 168

GLOSSARY 170

INDEX 174

INTRODUCTION

Welcome to the Edmonds Illustrated Cookbook.

Ninety years ago Edmonds published the first edition of a cookery book which featured 50 pages of economical and everyday recipes. This modest book captured the culinary imagination of New Zealanders and grew to become the indispensable cookbook for nearly every Kiwi household.

Almost a century later, the *Edmonds Illustrated Cookbook* celebrates the Edmonds' tradition with a selection of favourite recipes from yesteryear as well as capturing the essence of today's lifestyles with the introduction of some superb new classics.

This wonderfully illustrated book is designed to guide all cooks into the new millennium with the same emphasis as the original *Edmonds Cookery Book* on ease of preparation, economy and great tasting dishes the whole household can enjoy.

One of the joys of compiling this illustrated collection was the opportunity to photograph many of the favourite dishes from old editions of the standard *Edmonds Cookery Book*. Yet the challenge was to introduce new recipes that reflect influences from international cultures, café-style food, and the light and easy food that New Zealanders have come to enjoy. We are sure that readers will be inspired by the stunning photography to prepare many of the dishes featured.

With the Edmonds' heritage firmly established in family baking, the *Edmonds*

Illustrated Cookbook offers a fully comprehensive Baking section which includes chapters on buns, breads, muffins, cakes, biscuits and slices. Sections to cover every meal occasion complete the book: Light Meals and Home-Cooked Meals offer delicious fare from breakfasts to main courses; Desserts features chapters on both cold desserts and hot puddings and the traditional Preserves chapter completes the selection with some tasty spreads and pickles.

Tastes are changing as New Zealand comes into contact with international cultures and this diversity is bringing a new vibrance and informality to meal times.

However, it is reassuring to know that as the century draws to a close, the providing and sharing of food has not lost its importance in our daily lives. Edmonds recognises both the value of tradition and the desire for fresh approaches to food, and brings both together with this superb new selection of recipes.

We hope you enjoy cooking from this book as much as we enjoyed testing all the recipes.

The Edmonds' Team, April 1998

BAKING

BREADS & BUNS

BAGELS

2 teaspoons sugar
2 cups tepid water
1 tablespoon Edmonds active yeast
4 cups Champion high grade flour
1 teaspoon salt
1/4 cup sugar

EGG GLAZE
1 egg
1 tablespoon water

Dissolve first measure of sugar in water. Sprinkle over yeast and leave for about 10 minutes or until frothy. Put flour and salt in a bowl. Mix to combine. Pour in yeast mixture and mix until a stiff dough, adding more water if necessary. Knead dough until smooth and elastic. Place dough in a greased bowl. Turn dough over. Cover with plastic wrap and set aside in a warm place until double in bulk. Punch dough down. Form into a cylinder and break into 18 even-sized pieces. Roll each piece into a ball. Make a hole in the centre of the ball by pushing your finger through and spinning the dough around to make a large hole, the size of a small fist. Dust bagels with flour. Cover with a clean cloth. Set aside and leave to rise in a warm place for about 30 minutes. Dissolve second measure of sugar in a large saucepan of boiling water. Cook one bagel at a time in the boiling water for 30 seconds on each side. Remove with a slotted spoon. Drain and place on a greased baking tray. Brush well with egg glaze. Bake at 200°C for 15 to 20 minutes or until bagels sound hollow when tapped. Cool on a wire rack. *Makes 18.*

EGG GLAZE
Beat egg and water together.

CHELSEA BUNS

1 tablespoon sugar
1/2 cup tepid water
1 tablespoon Edmonds active yeast
1/2 cup milk
50 g butter
2 eggs
4 cups Champion high grade flour
25 g butter
1/2 cup brown sugar
1 teaspoon mixed spice
1/2 cup sultanas
1/2 cup currants

Dissolve first measure of sugar in water. Sprinkle over yeast. Leave for 10 minutes or until frothy. Scald milk. Add first measure of butter and stir until melted. Cool. Beat in eggs until combined. Place flour in a large bowl. Make a well in the centre. Pour in yeast and milk mixtures. Mix with a wooden spoon until combined. Turn onto a lightly floured board and knead until smooth and elastic. Place dough in a greased bowl. Turn dough over. Cover with plastic wrap and set aside in a warm place until double in bulk. Punch dough down. Turn onto a floured board and knead until smooth. Roll dough into a 35 cm square. Melt second measure of butter and use to brush dough liberally. Combine brown sugar, spice, sultanas and currants. Sprinkle over the dough and then roll up as for a Swiss roll. Cut into 2.5 cm slices. Place buns on a greased oven tray, close together but not touching. Cover with a clean cloth. Place in a warm place and leave to rise until buns are touching each other. Bake at 190°C for 30 to 35 minutes or until golden. Ice with white or pink icing (p. 168) if wished. Serve warm. *Makes 10.*

CORN BREAD

1 cup Champion standard
    plain flour
1 teaspoon salt
2 tablespoons Edmonds
    baking powder
2 teaspoons Mexican chilli powder

1 cup fine cornmeal
2 eggs
310 g can cream-style corn
½ cup milk
1 cup grated tasty cheese

Sift flour, salt, baking powder and chilli powder into a bowl. Mix in cornmeal. Mix eggs, corn and milk together. Pour into dry ingredients and mix quickly until just combined. Pour mixture into a 24 x 13 cm loaf tin lined on the base with baking paper. Sprinkle with grated cheese and bake at 180°C for 45 to 60 minutes or until an inserted skewer comes out clean. Cool in tin for 10 minutes before turning out onto a wire rack.

HOT CROSS BUNS

1½ cups milk
1 teaspoon sugar
2 tablespoons Edmonds
    active yeast
125 g butter, softened
¾ cup sugar
1 egg
¾ cup currants
½ cup sultanas
2 teaspoons mixed spice
1 teaspoon ground cinnamon
1 tablespoon mixed peel

6 – 7 cups Champion high
    grade flour

CROSSES
½ cup Champion standard
    plain flour
6 tablespoons water, approximately

GLAZE
1 tablespoon sugar
1 tablespoon water
1 teaspoon gelatine

Heat milk and sugar until lukewarm. Add yeast and leave to froth. Cream butter and sugar until light and fluffy. Add egg, currants, sultanas, mixed spice, cinnamon and peel. Sift 6 cups of flour into a large bowl. Add yeast and fruit mixture alternately and combine to a firm but pliable dough using more flour if necessary. Turn out onto a floured board and knead for 10 minutes. Place in a greased bowl and leave in a warm place to double in bulk. Punch down dough and shape ¼ cups of mixture into balls. Place side by side in two 20 x 30 cm greased sponge roll tins. Cover and leave to rise in a warm place until double in size. Pipe a cross on each bun. Bake at 200°C for 15 to 20 minutes or until golden. Remove from oven and brush with glaze. Cool hot cross buns on a wire rack. *Makes 18 buns.*

CROSSES
Mix flour and water together until smooth and able to be piped. Place mixture into a small plastic bag. Snip across one corner to form a hole for piping. Twist top of bag to hold mixture firm and squeeze to pipe.

GLAZE
Put all ingredients in a saucepan. Heat until sugar and gelatine have dissolved, stirring constantly.

FOCACCIA (ITALIAN BREAD)

1 teaspoon sugar
3/4 cup tepid water
1 tablespoon Edmonds active yeast
2 cups Champion high grade flour
1 tablespoon olive oil

TOPPING
olive oil
1 tablespoon dried rosemary
1 tablespoon rock salt

Dissolve sugar in water. Sprinkle over yeast. Leave for 10 minutes or until frothy. Place flour in a bowl. Make a well in the centre. Pour in yeast mixture and oil. Mix to a stiff dough. Turn onto a lightly floured board and knead until smooth and elastic. Place in a greased bowl. Turn dough over. Cover with plastic wrap and set aside in a warm place until double in bulk. Turn dough onto an oiled oven tray and roll to a 1.5 cm thick rectangle. Brush dough with olive oil. Sprinkle with rosemary and grind over rock salt. Dimple the surface of the dough with the fingertips. Cover with a clean cloth and leave in a warm place until doubled in bulk. Bake at 230°C for 15 to 20 minutes or until golden and cooked.

STOLLEN

1 teaspoon sugar
1/4 cup tepid water
1 tablespoon Edmonds active yeast
3/4 cup milk
1/4 cup sugar
100 g butter
1/2 teaspoon salt
3 1/2 cups Champion high grade flour

1 egg
2 cups mixed dried fruit
1/2 cup toasted almonds
1/4 cup brandy
200 g marzipan
melted butter
icing sugar

Dissolve first measure of sugar in water. Sprinkle over yeast. Set aside until frothy. Heat milk, second measure of sugar, butter and salt together. Cool. Add yeast to milk mixture. Beat 1 cup of the flour into milk mixture with a wooden spoon. Cover and set aside in a warm place until batter is bubbly. Beat egg and mix into batter with remaining flour. Mix dried fruit, almonds and brandy together. Mix into dough. Turn onto a lightly floured board and knead until smooth and elastic. Place in a greased bowl. Turn dough over and cover with plastic wrap. Set aside in a warm place until double in bulk. Punch dough down and knead lightly. Shape dough into a 20 x 30 cm rectangle on a greased oven tray. Roll marzipan into a 30 cm roll. Place marzipan one-third of the way from the dough's long edge. Fold the remaining two-thirds of the rectangle over the marzipan to within 5 cm of the long edge. Brush with melted butter. Cover with a clean cloth. Set aside in a warm place until double in bulk. If preferred, cut the mixture in half and make two smaller stollen. Bake at 200°C for 15 minutes. Reduce heat to 180°C and cook for 15 minutes or until stollen sounds hollow when tapped. Cool and dust with icing sugar.

MUFFINS LOAVES SCONES

BLUEBERRY MUFFINS

3 cups Champion standard
   plain flour
5 teaspoons Edmonds
   baking powder
¼ cup sugar

50 g butter
3 eggs
1½ cups milk
2 cups blueberries
icing sugar

Sift flour and baking powder into a bowl. Mix in sugar. Melt butter. Lightly beat eggs and milk together. Make a well in the centre of the dry ingredients. Add butter, milk mixture and blueberries. Mix quickly until just combined. Three-quarters fill greased muffin tins with mixture. Bake at 200°C for 15 minutes or until muffins spring back when lightly touched. Serve warm, dusted with icing sugar. **Makes 12.** *(Pictured below left.)*

BRAN MUFFINS

2 cups Champion standard
   plain flour
2 teaspoons Edmonds baking
   powder
1 teaspoon salt
1 teaspoon mixed spice
3 cups Fleming's bran flakes

½ cup brown sugar
2 eggs
2 teaspoons Edmonds baking soda
2 cups milk
2 tablespoons golden syrup
50 g butter
1 cup sultanas

Sift flour, baking powder, salt and mixed spice into a large bowl. Mix in bran and brown sugar. Make a well in the centre of the dry ingredients. Lightly beat eggs. Dissolve baking soda in milk. Melt golden syrup and butter together. Make a well in the centre of the dry ingredients. Add eggs, milk mixture, melted ingredients end sultanas. Mix quickly until just combined. Bake at 220°C for 15 minutes or until muffins spring back when lightly touched. **Makes 12.**

CORN, CHEESE AND BACON MUFFINS

2 rashers bacon, rind removed
2 cups Champion standard
*   plain flour*
5 teaspoons Edmonds
*   baking powder*
310 g can cream-style corn
2 eggs
1 cup milk
2 cups grated tasty cheese

Chop bacon into small pieces. Fry lightly and drain. Sift flour and baking powder into a bowl. Make a well in the centre. Mix corn, eggs, bacon and milk together. Pour corn mixture into dry ingredients and add half the cheese. Mix quickly until just combined. Three-quarters fill greased muffin tins with the mixture. Sprinkle with remaining cheese. Bake at 190°C for 20 minutes or until muffins spring back when lightly touched. **Makes 12.** *(Pictured below left.)*

DATE LOAF

1 cup chopped dates
1 cup boiling water
1 teaspoon Edmonds baking soda
1 tablespoon butter
1 cup brown sugar
1 egg
1 cup chopped walnuts
1/4 teaspoon vanilla essence
2 cups Champion standard
*   plain flour*
1 teaspoon Edmonds
*   baking powder*

Put dates, water, soda and butter into a bowl. Stir until butter has melted. Set aside for 1 hour. Beat sugar, egg, walnuts and vanilla into date mixture. Sift flour and baking powder into date mixture, stirring to just combine. Pour mixture into a 22 cm loaf tin lined on the base with baking paper. Bake at 180°C for 50 to 60 minutes or until loaf springs back when lightly touched. Leave in tin for 10 minutes before turning out onto a wire rack.

APRICOT LOAF
Replace dates with apricots.

GINGER GEMS

50 g butter, softened
1/2 cup sugar
2 teaspoons ground ginger
1 egg
2 tablespoons golden syrup

1 cup Champion standard
   plain flour
1 teaspoon Edmonds baking soda
1/2 cup milk
butter

Preheat gem irons in oven at 200°C. Cream butter, sugar and ginger in a bowl until light and fluffy. Add egg, beating well. Beat in golden syrup. Sift flour into creamed mixture. Stir to combine. Dissolve baking soda in milk. Quickly stir into creamed mixture. Place small pieces of butter into hot gem irons. Spoon mixture into irons. Bake at 200°C for 10 minutes or until well risen and golden brown. *Makes 12.*

PIKELETS

1 cup Champion standard
    plain flour
1 teaspoon Edmonds
    baking powder
¼ teaspoon salt
1 egg
¼ cup sugar
¾ cup milk, approximately

Sift flour, baking powder and salt into a bowl. In another bowl beat egg and sugar until thick. Add with milk to the sifted ingredients. Mix until just combined. Drop tablespoons of the mixture from the point of a spoon onto a hot greased griddle or non-stick frying pan. Turn pikelets over when bubbles start to burst on the top surface. Cook second side until golden. **Makes 15.**

SCONES

3 cups Champion standard
    plain flour
6 teaspoons Edmonds
    baking powder
¼ teaspoon salt
50 g butter
1¼ cups milk
milk

Sift flour, baking powder and salt into a bowl. Cut butter in until mixture resembles fine breadcrumbs. Add milk and mix quickly to a soft dough with a knife. Lightly knead. Lightly dust an oven tray with flour. Press scone dough out onto tray. Cut into 12 even-sized pieces. Leave a 2 cm space between scones. Brush tops with milk. Bake at 220°C for 10 minutes or until golden brown. **Makes 12.**

CHEESE SCONES
Add ½ cup grated cheese and a pinch of cayenne pepper to flour. Before baking, top each scone with a small amount of grated cheese.

DATE SCONES
Add ¾ cup chopped dates, 1 tablespoon sugar and ½ teaspoon cinnamon to flour. Before baking sprinkle scones with mixture of cinnamon and sugar.

SULTANA SCONES
Add ½ cup sultanas to flour.

CAKES

BANANA CAKE

125 g butter, softened
3/4 cup sugar
2 eggs
1 cup mashed bananas
1 teaspoon Edmonds baking soda
2 tablespoons hot milk
2 cups Champion standard plain flour
1 teaspoon Edmonds baking powder
Chocolate or Lemon Icing

Cream butter and sugar until light and fluffy. Add eggs one at a time, beating well after each addition. Add mashed banana and mix thoroughly. Stir baking soda into hot milk and add to creamed mixture. Sift flour and baking powder together. Stir into mixture. Turn into a 20 cm round cake tin lined on the base with baking paper. Bake at 180°C for 50 minutes or until cake springs back when lightly touched. Leave in tin for 10 minutes before turning out onto a wire rack. The mixture can also be baked in two 20 cm round sandwich tins at 180°C for 25 minutes. When cold ice with lemon or chocolate icing (p. 168) or dust with icing sugar. The two cakes can be filled with whipped cream and sliced banana. *(Main picture, middle left.)*

BOILED FRUIT CAKE

500 g mixed fruit
water
250 g butter
1 1/2 cups sugar
3 eggs, beaten
3 cups Champion standard plain flour
4 teaspoons Edmonds baking powder
1/2 teaspoon almond essence
1/2 teaspoon vanilla essence

Put mixed fruit in a large saucepan. Add just enough water to cover. Cover and bring to the boil. Remove from heat. Stir in butter and sugar, stirring constantly until butter has melted. Allow to cool. Beat in eggs. Sift flour and baking powder into fruit mixture, stirring to combine. Stir in almond and vanilla essences. Line a 23 cm square cake tin with two layers of brown paper followed by one layer of baking paper. Spoon mixture into cake tin. Bake at 160°C for 1 to 1 1/2 hours or until an inserted skewer comes out clean when tested. Leave in tin for 10 minutes before turning out onto a wire rack.
(Main picture, bottom.)

BUTTER CAKE

225 g butter, softened
1 1/2 teaspoons vanilla essence
1 1/4 cups sugar
3 eggs
2 1/4 cups Champion standard plain flour
4 1/2 teaspoons Edmonds baking powder
1 1/4 cups milk, approximately
icing sugar

Cream butter, vanilla and sugar until light and fluffy. Add eggs one at a time, beating well after each addition. Sift flour and baking powder together. Fold into creamed mixture. Add sufficient milk to give a soft dropping consistency. Spoon mixture into a deep 20 cm round cake tin lined on the base with baking paper. Bake at 180°C for 35 to 40 minutes or until cake springs back when lightly touched. Leave in tin for 10 minutes before turning out onto a wire rack. When cold dust with icing sugar.

LEMON SYRUP CAKE

Spoon mixture into a 22 cm loaf tin lined on the bottom with baking paper. After cooking cake, spoon hot syrup over hot cake. Leave in tin until cold.

SYRUP

3 tablespoons lemon juice
1/4 cup sugar

Gently heat lemon juice and sugar together, stirring until sugar has dissolved.

CAPPUCCINO CAKE

150 g butter
3/4 cup sugar
3 egg yolks
1 1/2 cups Champion
　standard plain flour
2 teaspoons Edmonds
　baking powder

1/2 cup strong black coffee
1 teaspoon cinnamon

TOPPING

3 egg whites
3/4 cup sugar

Melt butter in a saucepan large enough to mix all the ingredients. Remove from heat and stir in sugar and egg yolks. Fold in sifted flour and baking powder alternately with coffee. Place mixture in a 20 cm round cake tin lined on the bottom with baking paper. Spread topping over. Bake at 180°C for 45 to 50 minutes or until an inserted skewer comes out clean. Cool in tin before turning out onto a wire rack. Dust with cinnamon.

TOPPING

Beat egg whites until stiff. Gradually beat in sugar and continue beating until mixture is thick.

CHERRY ALMOND CAKE

1/2 cup ground almonds
butter, melted for greasing
200 g butter, softened
1 cup sugar
3 eggs
1 teaspoon almond essence

2 cups Champion standard
　plain flour
3 teaspoons Edmonds
　baking powder
3/4 cup milk
1 cup chopped glacé cherries

Sprinkle ground almonds over the base of a frying pan and heat gently until lightly golden. Grease a 22 cm fancy ring mould generously with melted butter. Toss almonds in tin to coat the base and sides. Cream second measure of butter and sugar until light and fluffy. Beat in eggs one at a time, beating well after each addition. Mix in almond essence. Sift flour and baking powder together. Fold into creamed mixture alternately with the milk. Mix in cherries. Spoon mixture into prepared tin. Bake at 160°C for 50 to 60 minutes or until cake springs back when lightly touched. Leave in tin for 10 minutes before turning out onto a wire rack. *(Pictured below left.)*

CARROT CAKE

3 eggs
1/2 cup oil
2 cups Champion standard
　plain flour
1 cup sugar
3 teaspoons Edmonds baking soda

1/2 teaspoon cinnamon
3 cups grated carrot
1/2 cup chopped walnuts
1 teaspoon grated orange rind
3/4 cup crushed pineapple
Cream Cheese Icing

Beat eggs until thick. Stir in oil. Sift flour, sugar, baking soda and cinnamon into the egg mixture. Stir to combine. Stir in carrots, walnuts, orange rind and pineapple. Line the base of a 23 cm ring tin with baking paper. Spoon mixture into tin. Bake at 180°C for 40 minutes or until cake springs back when lightly touched. Leave in tin for 10 minutes before turning out onto a wire rack. When cold ice with cream cheese icing (p. 168) if wished.

CHOCOLATE ÉCLAIRS & CREAM PUFFS

100 g butter
1 cup water
1 cup Champion standard
    plain flour

3 eggs
whipped cream
Chocolate Icing

Combine butter and water in a saucepan. Bring to a rolling boil. Remove from heat and quickly add flour. Beat with a wooden spoon until mixture leaves the sides of the saucepan. Allow to cool for 5 minutes. Add eggs one at a time, beating well after each addition, until mixture is glossy. Pipe 7 cm strips of the mixture onto greased oven trays. Bake at 200°C for 30 minutes or until éclairs are puffy and golden, then lower heat to 120°C and continue baking for about 15 minutes until dry. Cool thoroughly. Using a sharp knife, cut slits in the sides of each éclair. Fill with whipped cream and ice tops with chocolate icing (p. 168). **Makes 30.**

CREAM PUFFS

Pipe or spoon small teaspoons of mixture onto greased oven trays. Bake as above. Cool thoroughly. Fill with whipped cream and ice tops with chocolate icing (p. 168) or dust with sifted icing sugar. **Makes 30.**

CHOCOLATE LOG

3 eggs
1/2 cup sugar
1/2 teaspoon vanilla essence
2 tablespoons cocoa
1/4 cup Champion standard
  plain flour
1 teaspoon Edmonds
  baking powder

25 g butter, melted
1 tablespoon water
icing sugar
raspberry jam
whipped cream
Chocolate Icing

Beat eggs, sugar and vanilla until thick. Sift cocoa, flour and baking powder together. Add to egg mixture and fold in butter and water. Pour mixture into a 20 x 30 cm sponge roll tin lined on the base with baking paper. Bake at 190°C for 10 to 12 minutes or until cake springs back when lightly touched. When cooked turn onto baking paper sprinkled with sifted icing sugar. Spread with jam and roll from the short side immediately, using the paper to help. Leave the roll wrapped in the paper until cold, then unroll, fill with whipped cream and re-roll gently. Ice with chocolate icing (p. 168) and pipe with a shell pattern icing tube to resemble a log.

CHRISTMAS CAKE

1 3/4 cups orange juice
3/4 cup dark rum or brandy
2 tablespoons grated orange rind
500 g currants
500 g raisins
2 cups sultanas
2 cups chopped dates
150 g crystallised ginger, chopped
150 g packet mixed peel
150 g packet glacé cherries, halved
1/2 teaspoon vanilla essence
1/4 teaspoon almond essence

2 teaspoons grated lemon rind
1 cup blanched almonds
2 1/2 cups Champion high
  grade flour
1/2 teaspoon Edmonds baking soda
1 teaspoon cinnamon
1 teaspoon mixed spice
1/2 teaspoon ground nutmeg
250 g butter, softened
1 1/2 cups brown sugar
2 tablespoons treacle
5 eggs

In a saucepan, bring to the boil orange juice, rum and orange rind. Remove from heat and add dried fruit. Cover and leave fruit to soak overnight. Stir vanilla and almond essences, lemon rind and almonds into saucepan. Sift flour, soda and spices into a bowl. In a separate large bowl, cream butter, sugar and treacle until light and fluffy. Add eggs one at a time, beating well after each addition. Into this mixture fold sifted ingredients alternately with fruit mixture. Line a deep, square 23 cm tin with two layers of brown paper followed by one layer of baking paper. Spoon mixture into tin. Bake at 150°C for 4 hours or until an inserted skewer comes out clean when tested. Leave in tin until cold. Wrap in foil. Store in a cool place. Ice if wished.

CHRISTMAS MINCE PIES

400 g Sweet Shortcrust Pastry (p. 169)
1 cup Christmas mincemeat
1 egg, beaten
icing sugar

On a lightly floured board roll out pastry to 3 mm thickness. Cut out rounds using a 7 cm cutter, and use to line about 16 patty tins. Using a 6 cm round cutter, cut out tops from the remaining pastry. Spoon teaspoons of mincemeat into each base. Brush the edges of the bases with some of the egg. Place tops over the filling, pressing slightly around the edges to seal the pies. Glaze with the remaining beaten egg. Bake at 180°C for 15 minutes or until lightly browned. To serve, heat at 140°C for 15 minutes or until warm. Dust with sifted icing sugar. **Makes 16.**

CHRISTMAS MINCEMEAT

2 medium apples, unpeeled,
  quartered and cored
100 g suet
1 1/4 cups currants
1 1/4 cups sultanas
1 1/4 cups raisins
1 1/4 cups mixed peel
1/4 cup blanched almonds
1 cup brown sugar
1/4 teaspoon salt
1/2 teaspoon ground nutmeg
2 tablespoons brandy or whisky or
  lemon juice

Mince or finely chop apples, suet, currants, sultanas, raisins, peel and almonds. Add sugar, salt, nutmeg and brandy. Mix well. Spoon mixture into clean jars and seal. If using lemon juice, refrigerate. **Makes 6 cups.**

LIGHT CHRISTMAS MINCEMEAT
Delete suet and store mincemeat in refrigerator.

CINNAMON CREAM OYSTERS OR FINGERS

2 eggs
1/4 cup sugar
2 teaspoons golden syrup
6 tablespoons Champion standard plain flour
1/2 teaspoon Edmonds baking powder
1/4 teaspoon Edmonds baking soda
1 teaspoon cinnamon
1/2 teaspoon ground ginger
whipped cream

Beat eggs and sugar until thick. Add golden syrup and beat well. Sift flour, baking powder, baking soda, cinnamon and ginger together. Fold dry ingredients into egg mixture. Spoon small amounts of mixture into greased sponge oyster or sponge finger tins. Bake at 200°C for 10 to 12 minutes or until the surface springs back when lightly touched. When cold cut oysters open with a sharp knife and fill with whipped cream. **Makes 16.** *(Pictured below left.)*

CONTINENTAL APPLE CAKE

250 g butter, melted
1 1/4 cups sugar
3 1/4 cups Champion standard plain flour
6 teaspoons Edmonds baking powder
4 eggs
2 large Granny Smith apples, sliced
1/2 cup sultanas
2 tablespoons sugar
2 teaspoons cinnamon
1 teaspoon almond essence
icing sugar
whipped cream or yoghurt

Put butter, first measure of sugar, flour, baking powder and eggs into a bowl. Beat with an electric mixer on high speed until smooth. In a separate bowl combine apple slices, sultanas, second measure of sugar, cinnamon and almond essence. Spoon two-thirds of the batter into a 25 cm round cake tin lined on the base with baking paper. Arrange the apple mixture on top. Spoon remaining batter over apple mixture. Bake at 180°C for 1 1/4 hours or until cake springs back when lightly touched. Leave in tin for 10 minutes before turning out onto a wire rack.

ECCLES CAKES

50 g butter, softened
½ cup brown sugar
¼ cup candied peel
1½ cups currants

1 teaspoon cinnamon
a little grated nutmeg
400 g packet flaky pastry
extra sugar

Cream the butter and sugar. Stir in peel, currants, cinnamon and nutmeg. Roll pastry out to 2 mm thickness and cut into rounds 10 cm in diameter. Put 1 tablespoon of the fruit mixture on centre of each, wet the edges and pinch them together to form a ball. Turn over and flatten until the currants show through. Brush top with water. Cut two slashes in each top, sprinkle with sugar and bake at 220°C for 15 minutes or until golden. **Makes 18.**

FIELDER'S SPONGE

3 eggs, separated
3/4 cup caster sugar
3/4 cup Edmonds Fielder's
   cornflour
1 tablespoon Champion
   standard plain flour

1 teaspoon Edmonds
   baking powder
2 teaspoons golden syrup
1 tablespoon boiling water

Beat egg whites until stiff. Beat in sugar, then yolks. Sift cornflour, flour and baking powder into egg mixture. Add golden syrup dissolved in boiling water and mix gently with a metal spoon. Pour into two 20 cm sandwich tins lined on the base with baking paper. Bake at 190°C for 20 minutes or until cake springs back when lightly touched. Leave in tin for 5 minutes before turning out onto a wire rack. *(Pictured below left.)*

GINGER KISSES

50 g butter
1/2 cup sugar
1 tablespoon golden syrup
2 eggs
1 1/4 cups Champion standard
   plain flour
1 teaspoon Edmonds
   baking powder

1 teaspoon cinnamon
2 teaspoons ground ginger

MOCK CREAM
25g butter
1/4 cup icing sugar
3 tablespoons boiling water

In a saucepan melt butter, sugar and golden syrup. Beat eggs until thick and mix in alternately with sifted flour, baking powder, cinnamon and ginger. Bake small spoonfuls on greased trays at 200°C for 10 to 12 minutes. Put together with mock cream. ***Makes 10.***

MOCK CREAM
Put ingredients in a bowl and beat with electric beater until thick and of a cream consistency. If the mixture should curdle, keep on beating until smooth.

GINGERBREAD

125 g butter, softened
1/2 cup brown sugar
1 cup golden syrup
1 egg
2 1/2 cups Champion standard
  plain flour
1/4 teaspoon salt
1 1/2 teaspoons Edmonds
  baking soda
1 1/2 teaspoons ground ginger
1 teaspoon cinnamon
3/4 cup milk

Cream butter and sugar in a bowl until light and fluffy. Warm golden syrup slightly until runny. Beat into creamed mixture. Add egg. Beat well. Sift flour, salt, baking soda, ginger and cinnamon together. Stir into creamed mixture alternately with milk. Pour mixture into a 23 cm square cake tin lined on the base with baking paper. Bake at 180°C for 55 to 60 minutes. Leave in tin for 10 minutes before turning out onto a wire rack. *(Main picture, top.)*

LADYSMITH CAKE

175 g butter, softened
3/4 cup sugar
3 eggs
1 1/2 cups Champion
  standard plain flour
1 teaspoon Edmonds
  baking powder
2 teaspoons cinnamon
1/4 cup raspberry jam
1/4 cup chopped nuts

Cream butter and sugar until light and fluffy. In a separate bowl beat eggs until thick. Sift flour and baking powder together. Add to creamed mixture alternately with the eggs. Transfer one-third of the mixture to a bowl. Stir in cinnamon. Reserve the remaining mixture. Spoon cinnamon mixture into an 18 cm square cake tin lined on the base with baking paper. Spread surface with raspberry jam. Top with reserved mixture. Sprinkle the top with chopped nuts. Bake at 180°C for 50 minutes or until cake springs back when lightly touched. Leave in tin for 10 minutes before turning out onto a wire rack. *(Main picture, middle.)*

LAMINGTONS

200 g sponge
Chocolate Icing
coconut

CHOCOLATE ICING
2 tablespoons cocoa
6 tablespoons boiling water
25 g butter, melted
2 1/4 cups icing sugar
1/4 teaspoon vanilla essence

Make or purchase sponge the day before required. Cut sponge into 4 cm squares. Dip each square in the chocolate icing. Roll in coconut. Leave to dry. **Makes 20.**

CHOCOLATE ICING
Dissolve cocoa in boiling water and combine with the butter. Sift icing sugar into a bowl. Add cocoa mixture. Add vanilla and stir until well combined.

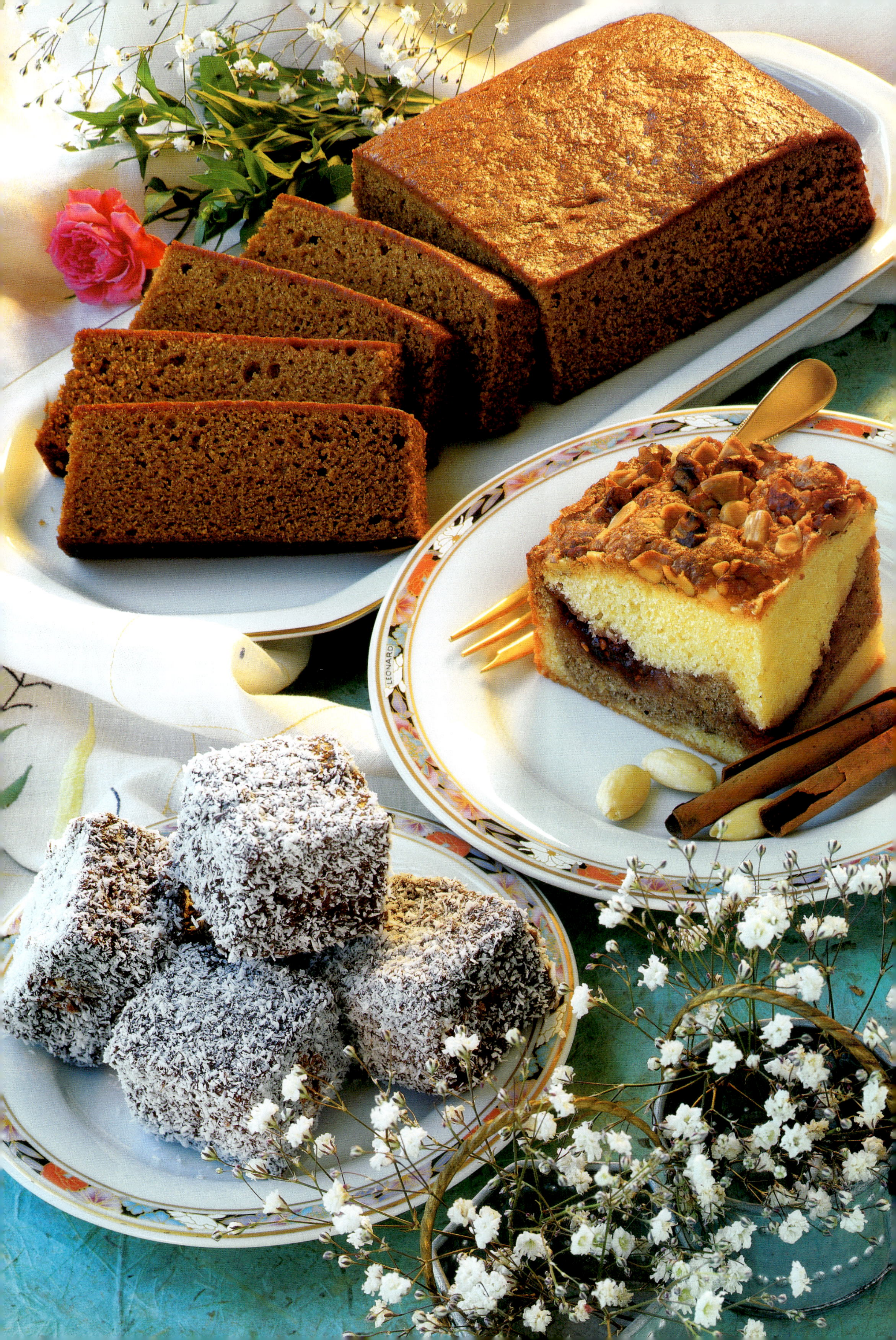

LIGHT FRUIT CAKE WITH TOFFEE NUTS

200 g butter, softened
1 1/2 cups sugar
4 eggs
1 teaspoon vanilla essence
2 cups Champion standard
   plain flour
3 teaspoons Edmonds
   baking powder

3/4 cup milk
1 cup sultanas
1 cup currants
400 g packet almond-flavoured icing
1 cup whole mixed roasted nuts

CARAMELISED SUGAR
1 cup sugar

Cream butter and sugar until light and fluffy. Beat in eggs one at a time, beating well after each addition. Mix in vanilla essence. Sift flour and baking powder into mixture and fold in with milk, sultanas and currants. Place mixture into a 20 cm square deep cake tin lined on the base with baking paper. Bake at 180°C for 1 hour or until an inserted skewer comes out clean. Cool in tin for 10 minutes before turning onto a wire rack. When cake is cold, roll almond icing to a 20 cm square. Trim icing edges to straighten. Place on top of inverted cake. Arrange nuts on almond icing and pour over caramelised sugar.

CARAMELISED SUGAR
Heat sugar gently in a heavy frying pan until it melts and starts to colour. Do not stir.

MACAROON CAKE

100 g butter
1/2 cup sugar
3 egg yolks
1 1/2 cups Champion standard
    plain flour
2 teaspoons Edmonds
    baking powder
1/2 cup milk
1 teaspoon vanilla essence
1/2 cup raspberry jam

TOPPING
3 egg whites
3/4 cup sugar
1 1/2 cups coconut
1 teaspoon almond essence

Melt butter in a saucepan large enough to mix all the ingredients. Stir in sugar and egg yolks. Sift flour and baking powder into the saucepan. Add milk and vanilla essence and mix with a wooden spoon to combine. Spread mixture into a 20 cm ring tin lined on the base with baking paper. A springform pan or loose-bottom cake tin is best. Spread jam over batter. Spread topping over. Bake at 180°C for 45 to 50 minutes or until an inserted skewer comes out clean. Cool in tin for 10 minutes before quickly inverting onto a wire rack covered with a clean teatowel, then turning onto another rack so topping does not get broken.

TOPPING
Beat egg whites until stiff. Gradually beat in sugar and continue beating until mixture is thick. Mix in coconut and almond essence.

MADEIRA CAKE

250 g butter, softened
1 cup sugar
1/2 teaspoon grated lemon rind
4 eggs
2 1/4 cups Champion standard
    plain flour
1 1/2 teaspoons Edmonds
    baking powder

Cream butter and sugar until light and fluffy. Stir in lemon rind. In a separate bowl beat eggs until thick. Sift flour and baking powder together. Add to creamed mixture alternately with the eggs. Stir to mix. Spoon mixture into a 20 cm square cake tin lined on the base with baking paper. Bake at 180°C for 30 minutes or until the cake springs back when lightly touched. Leave in tin for 10 minutes before turning out onto a wire rack.

MUD CAKE

BASE
200 g packet chocolate thin biscuits
75 g butter
1/2 cup chocolate hazelnut spread

CAKE
50 g butter
1 cup sugar
3 eggs
1 tablespoon vanilla essence

1 1/2 cups Champion standard
   plain flour
3 teaspoons Edmonds baking powder
3 tablespoons cocoa
1/4 cup boiling water
1/4 cup milk
icing sugar
Chocolate Sauce

BASE
Crush biscuits into fine crumbs. Melt butter and mix into biscuit crumbs. Press into the base of a 20 cm round cake tin lined on the base with baking paper. Spread with hazelnut spread. Pour over cake mixture. Bake at 180°C for 45 to 50 minutes or until cake springs back when lightly touched. Cool in tin for 10 minutes before turning out onto a wire rack. Dust with icing sugar and serve with ready-made chocolate sauce.

CAKE
Melt butter in a saucepan large enough to mix all the ingredients. Remove from heat. Mix in sugar, eggs and vanilla. Mix until combined. Sift flour and baking powder together. Mix cocoa into boiling water. Fold into butter mixture with sifted ingredients and milk. *(Pictured below left.)*

ONE-EGG CHOCOLATE CAKE

50 g butter
1 tablespoon golden syrup
1 egg
1/2 cup sugar
1 tablespoon cocoa
1 cup Champion standard
   plain flour

1 teaspoon Edmonds
   baking powder
few drops vanilla essence
1 teaspoon Edmonds baking soda
3/4 cup milk
Chocolate Icing

Melt butter and golden syrup in a saucepan large enough to mix all ingredients. Add egg and sugar and beat well. Sift cocoa, flour and baking powder together. Fold sifted ingredients and vanilla into egg mixture. Dissolve baking soda in milk. Fold into egg mixture. Pour mixture into two 20 cm sponge sandwich tins lined on the base with baking paper. Bake at 190°C for 30 minutes or until cake springs back when lightly touched. Leave in tin for 5 minutes before turning out onto a wire rack. When cold ice with chocolate icing (p. 168).

ORANGE CAKE

175 g butter, softened
3/4 cup sugar
2 teaspoons grated orange rind
3 eggs
1 1/4 cups Champion standard
  plain flour

1 teaspoon Edmonds
  baking powder
Orange Icing

Cream butter and sugar, add orange rind. Beat eggs until thick and add alternately with sifted flour and baking powder. Pour into a 20 cm ring tin lined on the base with baking paper. Bake at 180°C for about 40 minutes or until cake springs back when lightly touched. Cool in tin for 10 minutes before turning out onto a wire rack. When cold ice with orange icing (p. 168).
(Pictured below left.)

TENNIS CAKE

175 g butter, softened
1 1/2 cups sugar
1/2 teaspoon vanilla essence
1/2 teaspoon almond essence
2 cups Champion standard
  plain flour
1/4 teaspoon cinnamon

1 teaspoon Edmonds
  baking powder
4 eggs, beaten
3/4 cup raisins
1/2 cup chopped glacé cherries
2 teaspoons grated lemon rind
2 tablespoons lemon juice

Cream butter and sugar until light and fluffy. Add vanilla and almond essences. Sift flour, cinnamon and baking powder together. Add eggs alternately with sifted dry ingredients. Mix in raisins, cherries, lemon rind and juice. Spoon mixture into a 22 cm round cake tin lined on the base with baking paper. Bake at 160°C for 1 to 1 1/2 hours or until an inserted skewer comes out clean when tested. Leave in tin for 10 minutes before turning out onto a wire rack.

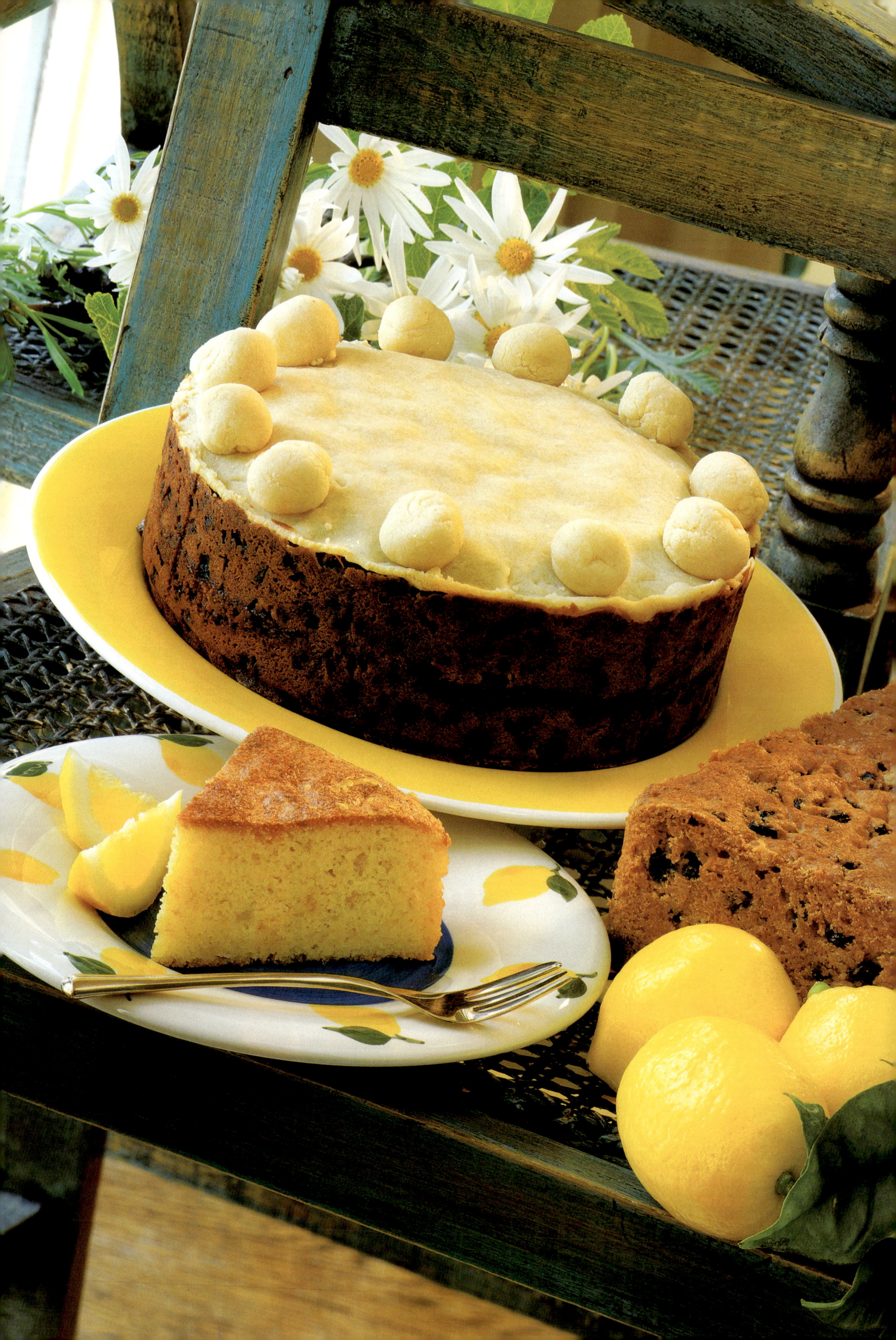

SEMOLINA CAKE

*3 tablespoons Champion standard
   plain flour*
3/4 cup Fleming's semolina
4 eggs
1/2 cup sugar
1 tablespoon grated lemon rind

SYRUP

1 cup sugar
1/2 cup water
1/4 cup lemon juice
1 teaspoon grated lemon rind

In a bowl combine flour and semolina. Separate the eggs. Beat egg yolks and sugar together until pale and thick. Gently fold semolina mixture and lemon rind into egg mixture. Beat egg whites until stiff but not dry. Fold a quarter of egg whites into egg mixture, then remaining egg whites. Pour mixture into a 20 cm springform tin lined on the base with baking paper. Bake at 180°C for 40 minutes or until skewer comes out clean when tested. Leave in tin 10 minutes before transferring to a serving plate. Pour hot syrup over cake about a quarter at a time, leaving time for the cake to soak up syrup.

SYRUP

Place sugar, water, lemon juice and rind in a small saucepan. Heat gently, stirring constantly until sugar has dissolved. *(Main picture, bottom left.)*

SULTANA CAKE

2 cups sultanas
water
*250 g butter, chopped in
   small pieces*
1 cup sugar
3 eggs, beaten
*1/2 teaspoon lemon essence
   or almond essence*
*3 cups Champion standard
   plain flour*
*1 1/2 teaspoons Edmonds
   baking powder*

Put sultanas in a saucepan. Cover with water. Bring to the boil then simmer for 15 minutes. Drain thoroughly. Add butter. In a bowl beat sugar into eggs until well combined. Add sultana mixture and essence. Sift flour and baking powder together. Mix sifted ingredients into fruit mixture. Spoon mixture into a 20 cm square cake tin lined on the base with baking paper. Bake at 160°C for 1 1/4 to 1 1/2 hours or until cake springs back when lightly touched. Leave in tin for 10 minutes before turning out onto a wire rack.

(Main picture, bottom right.)

SIMNEL CAKE

500 g marzipan
icing sugar
250 g butter, softened
1 cup sugar
4 eggs
*2 1/2 cups Champion standard
   plain flour*
*1 teaspoon Edmonds
   baking powder*
1 1/2 cups sultanas
1 1/2 cups currants
1/2 cup mixed peel
1/2 cup chopped glacé cherries

Cut marzipan into thirds. Using two of the marzipan pieces, roll out two rounds on greaseproof paper dusted with icing sugar to fit a 22 cm round cake tin. Cream butter and sugar until light and fluffy. Beat in eggs one at a time, beating well after each addition. Sift flour and baking powder together. Mix in sultanas, currants, peel and cherries. Fold into creamed mixture. Spoon half the mixture into the cake tin lined on the base with baking paper, spreading the mixture evenly. Cover with one of the marzipan rounds, then spread remaining cake mixture on top and smooth. Bake at 150°C for 2 hours. Reduce heat to 130°C and bake for a further 1/2 to 1 hour or until an inserted skewer comes out clean. While cake is cooking, use the unrolled marzipan to make 11 balls. Place the second marzipan round on top of the hot cake and decorate with the 11 balls. Return the cake to the oven for about 15 minutes until the marzipan is lightly browned. Leave to cool in tin.

BISCUITS

AFGHANS

200 g butter, softened
1/2 cup sugar
1 1/4 cups Champion standard
   plain flour
3 tablespoons cocoa
1 1/2 cups cornflakes
Chocolate Icing
walnuts (optional)

Cream butter and sugar until light and fluffy. Sift flour and cocoa. Stir into creamed mixture. Fold in cornflakes. Spoon mounds of mixture onto a greased oven tray, gently pressing the mixture together. Bake at 180°C for 15 minutes or until set. When cold, ice with chocolate icing (p. 168) and decorate with a walnut if wished. *Makes 20.*
(Pictured below left.)

ALMOND BISCUITS

125 g butter, softened
1/2 cup sugar
1 egg
1/2 teaspoon almond essence
1 1/2 cups Champion standard
   plain flour
1 teaspoon Edmonds
   baking powder
18 blanched almonds

Cream butter and sugar until light and fluffy. Add egg and almond essence, beating well. Sift in flour and baking powder. Mix to a firm dough. Roll into small balls. Place on a greased oven tray. Press half a blanched almond on each. Bake at 180°C for 15 minutes or until cooked. *Makes 36.*

ANZAC BISCUITS

1/2 cup Champion standard
   plain flour
1/2 cup sugar
3/4 cup coconut
3/4 cup Fleming's rolled oats

75 g butter
1 tablespoon golden syrup
1/2 teaspoon Edmonds baking soda
2 tablespoons boiling water

Mix together flour, sugar, coconut and rolled oats. Melt butter and golden syrup. Dissolve baking soda in the boiling water and add to butter and golden syrup. Stir butter mixture into the dry ingredients. Place level tablespoons of mixture onto cold greased trays. Press out with a fork. Bake at 180°C for about 15 minutes or until golden. *Makes 18.* *(Main picture, bottom.)*

BELGIUM BISCUITS

125 g butter, softened
1/4 cup brown sugar
1 egg
2 cups Champion standard
　plain flour
1 teaspoon Edmonds
　baking powder
1 teaspoon cinnamon
1 teaspoon ground ginger
1 teaspoon mixed spice
1 teaspoon cocoa

ICING
3/4 to 1 cup icing sugar
1/4 teaspoon raspberry or
　vanilla essence
few drops red food colouring
water

FILLING
1/2 cup raspberry jam,
　approximately

Cream butter and sugar until light and fluffy. Add egg and beat well. Sift flour, baking powder, cinnamon, ginger, mixed spice and cocoa together. Mix into creamed mixture to make a firm dough. On a lightly floured board roll dough out to 3 mm thickness. Cut out rounds using a 6.5 cm cutter. Arrange on greased oven tray and bake at 180°C for 15 minutes or until golden. When cold, ice half the biscuits. Spread the un-iced biscuits with raspberry jam and place iced biscuits on top. **Makes 18.**

ICING
Mix icing sugar with essence and colouring. Add sufficient water to make a pink spreadable icing.

BISCOTTI

2 cups Champion standard
   plain flour
2 teaspoons Edmonds
   baking powder
pinch of salt

1/2 cup caster sugar
1 teaspoon almond essence
3 eggs
1/2 cup chopped, toasted almonds

Sift flour, baking powder and salt into a bowl. Mix in caster sugar. Lightly beat almond essence and eggs together. Mix into dry ingredients with almonds until well combined. The dough should be firm. Add more flour if necessary. Shape into a log about 30 cm long. Place on a greased oven tray and flatten the log with the palm of your hand. Bake at 180°C for 35 minutes or until cooked. Cool then cut log into 1 cm slices on the diagonal. Place slices on an oven tray. Bake at 150°C for 10 minutes or until biscotti are dry and crisp. Store in an airtight container. **Makes approx. 40.** *(Pictured below left.)*

BRANDY SNAPS

1 teaspoon ground ginger
3 tablespoons golden syrup
1/2 cup sugar

75 g butter
1/2 cup Champion standard
   plain flour

Put ginger, golden syrup, sugar and butter in a saucepan. Heat gently until butter has melted, stirring occasionally. Remove from heat and allow to cool slightly. Sift flour into saucepan. Stir to combine. Drop tablespoons of mixture onto a greased oven tray, no more than four at a time. Allow room for spreading. Bake at 180°C for 8 minutes or until golden. Cool slightly until able to be removed from tray without collapsing. Remove hot brandy snaps with a spatula and wrap around the handle of wooden spoon to shape. You will probably fit two on one handle. Cool slightly and slide off. Leave until set. **Makes 12.**

DUSKIES

125 g butter, softened
1 cup icing sugar
1 egg
1 ¼ cups Champion standard
    plain flour
2 tablespoons cocoa

1 teaspoon Edmonds
    baking powder
½ cup desiccated coconut
½ cup chopped walnuts
Chocolate Icing

Cream butter and sugar, add egg then beat. Sift in flour, cocoa and baking powder. Add coconut and walnuts. Mix and place in small spoonfuls on cold, greased trays. Bake at 200°C for 12 to 15 minutes. When cold, ice with chocolate icing (p. 168) and decorate with desiccated coconut. *Makes 36.*

FLORENTINES

125 g butter, softened
1/2 cup sugar
5 tablespoons golden syrup
1/4 cup Champion standard
   plain flour
70 g packet sliced almonds

1/2 cup chopped glacé cherries
1/2 cup chopped walnuts
1/4 cup chopped mixed peel

ICING
150 g cooking chocolate

Cream butter and sugar. Beat in golden syrup. Sift in flour. Add almonds, cherries, walnuts and peel. Mix well. Place tablespoons of mixture on trays lined with baking paper, spacing them well apart to allow for spreading. Cook four at a time. Press each one out as flat and round as possible, using a knife. Bake at 180°C for 10 minutes or until golden brown. Remove from oven and leave on tray for 5 minutes before transferring to a wire rack. When cold ice with chocolate on the flat side of biscuit. **Makes 20.** *(Pictured below left.)*

ICING
Melt chocolate in a bowl over hot water.

HOKEY POKEY BISCUITS

125 g butter
1/2 cup sugar
1 tablespoon golden syrup
1 tablespoon milk

1 1/2 cups Champion standard
   plain flour
1 teaspoon Edmonds baking soda

Combine butter, sugar, golden syrup and milk in a saucepan. Heat until butter is melted and mixture nearly boiling, stirring constantly. Remove from heat and allow mixture to cool to lukewarm. Sift flour and baking soda together. Add to the cooled mixture. Stir well. Roll tablespoons of mixture into balls and place on ungreased oven trays. Flatten with a floured fork. Bake at 180°C for 15 to 20 minutes or until golden brown. **Makes 22.**

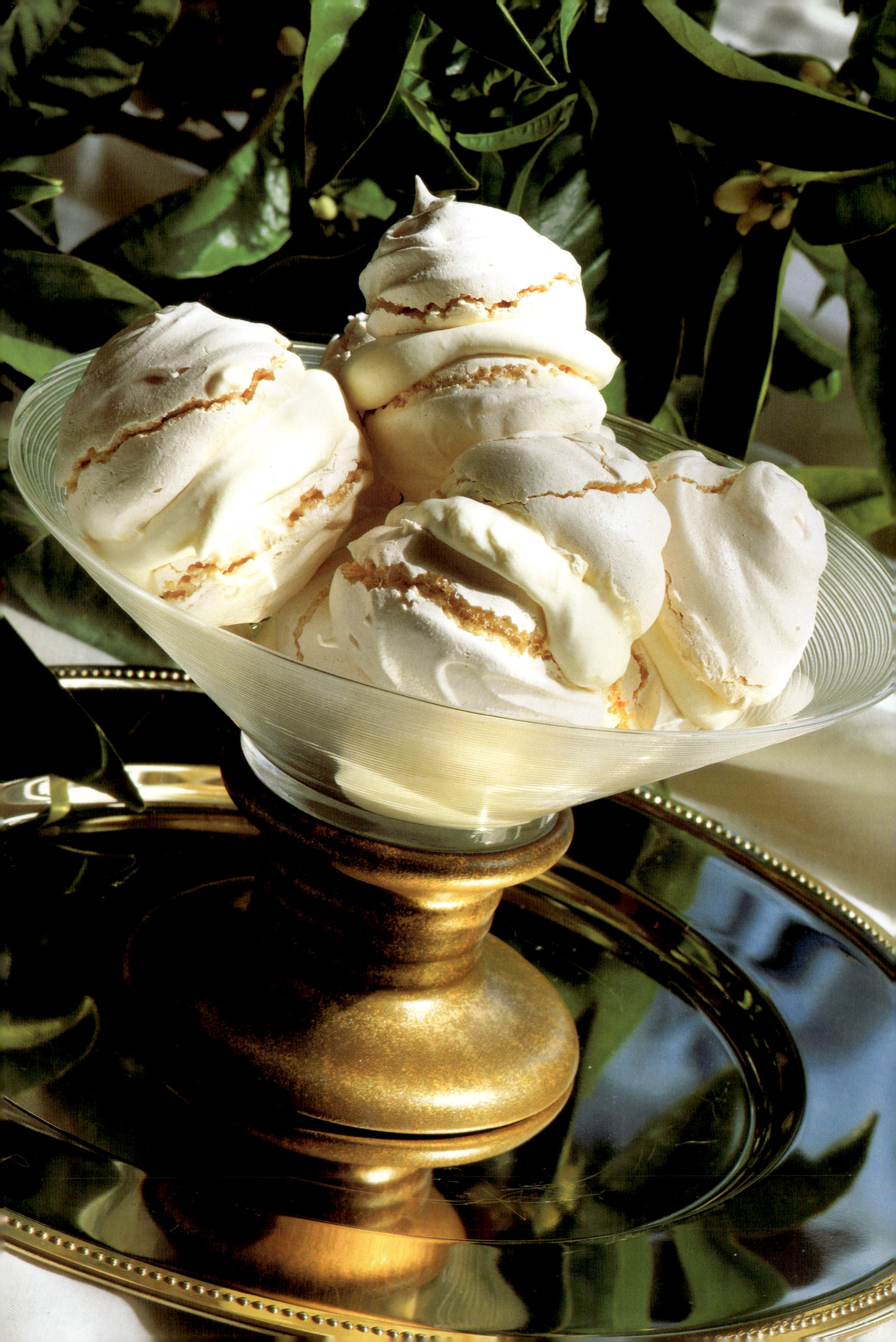

MERINGUES

2 egg whites
½ cup sugar
whipped cream

Beat egg whites until stiff but not dry. Add half the sugar and beat well. Repeat with remaining sugar. Beat until thick and glossy. Pipe or spoon small amounts of meringue onto a greased oven tray. Bake at 120°C for 1 to 1 ½ hours or until the meringues are dry but not brown. Cool and when required to serve, sandwich meringues together in pairs with whipped cream. Store unfilled meringues in an airtight container. ***Makes 12.*** *(Main picture.)*

MELTING MOMENTS

200 g butter, softened
¾ cup icing sugar
1 cup Champion standard
 plain flour
1 cup Edmonds Fielder's
 cornflour
½ teaspoon Edmonds
 baking powder
Butter Icing or raspberry jam

Cream butter and icing sugar until light and fluffy. Sift flour, cornflour and baking powder together. Add to creamed mixture, mixing well. Roll dough into small balls the size of large marbles and place on a greased oven tray. Flatten slightly with a floured fork. Bake at 180°C for 20 minutes or until cooked. Cool and sandwich two biscuits together with butter icing (p. 168) or raspberry jam. ***Makes 16.***

OAT BISCUITS

125 g butter, softened
½ cup sugar
2 tablespoons honey
1 cup Champion standard
 plain flour
1 teaspoon Edmonds
 baking powder
½ teaspoon cinnamon
1 ½ cups Fleming's rolled oats

Cream butter, sugar and honey together until pale. Sift flour, baking powder and cinnamon together. Add sifted dry ingredients and rolled oats to creamed mixture, stirring well. Roll tablespoons of mixture into balls. Place on a greased oven tray. Flatten with a floured fork and bake at 180°C for 15 minutes or until golden. Transfer to a wire rack to cool. ***Makes 30.***

PEANUT BROWNIES

125 g butter, softened
1 cup sugar
1 egg
1 1/2 cups Champion standard
　plain flour
1 teaspoon Edmonds
　baking powder
pinch of salt
2 tablespoons cocoa
1 cup peanuts, roasted and husked

Cream butter and sugar until light and fluffy. Add egg and beat well. Sift flour, baking powder, salt and cocoa together. Mix into creamed mixture. Add cold peanuts and mix well. Roll tablespoons of mixture into balls. Place on greased oven trays. Flatten with a floured fork. Bake at 180°C for 15 minutes or until cooked. **Makes 20.** *(Pictured below left.)*

SANTÉ BISCUITS

125 g butter, softened
1/4 cup sugar
3 tablespoons sweetened
　condensed milk
few drops vanilla essence
1 1/2 cups Champion standard
　plain flour
1 teaspoon Edmonds
　baking powder
1/2 cup chocolate chips

Cream butter, sugar, condensed milk and vanilla until light and fluffy. Sift flour and baking powder together. Mix sifted dry ingredients and chocolate chips into creamed mixture. Roll tablespoons of mixture into balls. Place on a greased oven tray and flatten with a floured fork. Bake at 180°C for 20 minutes. **Makes 25.**

SHORTBREAD

250 g butter, softened
1 cup icing sugar
1 cup Edmonds Fielder's cornflour
2 cups Champion standard
   plain flour
¼ teaspoon salt

Cream butter and icing sugar until light and fluffy. Add sifted cornflour, flour and salt to creamed mixture. Knead mixture and form into a long loaf measuring 5 cm across and 2 cm in depth. Cover with plastic wrap and place in refrigerator. When required, cut into 1.5 cm thick slices or less and place on a cold greased baking tray. Bake at 180°C for 15 to 20 minutes. **Makes 24.** *(Pictured below left.)*

YOYOS

175 g butter, softened
¼ cup icing sugar
few drops vanilla essence
1 ½ cups Champion standard
   plain flour
¼ cup Edmonds custard powder

BUTTER FILLING
75 g butter, softened
¾ cup icing sugar
3 tablespoons Edmonds
   custard powder

Cream butter and icing sugar until light and fluffy. Add vanilla. Sift flour and custard powder together. Mix sifted ingredients into creamed mixture. Roll teaspoons of mixture into balls. Place on a greased oven tray. Flatten with a floured fork. Bake at 180°C for 15 to 20 minutes. When cold sandwich together in pairs with butter filling. **Makes 26.**

BUTTER FILLING
Beat all ingredients together until well combined.

SLICES

APPLE SHORTCAKE SQUARES

2 cups Champion standard
　plain flour
1 teaspoon Edmonds
　baking powder
125 g butter
1/4 cup sugar
1 egg, beaten
1 to 2 tablespoons milk
575 g can 100% apple
icing sugar

Sift flour and baking powder into a bowl. Cut in butter until mixture resembles coarse breadcrumbs. Mix in first measure of sugar and the egg. Add sufficient milk to form a firm dough. Knead until smooth. Divide dough in half and roll out each piece to fit a 20 cm square cake tin lined on the base with baking paper. Place one piece of dough in tin and spread apple over it. Lightly press remaining dough on top. Bake at 180°C for 25 minutes. When cold sprinkle with sifted icing sugar and cut into squares.

CARAMEL MERINGUE

BASE
75 g butter, softened
1 1/2 tablespoons sugar
1 egg
1 cup Champion standard
　plain flour
1 teaspoon Edmonds
　baking powder
pinch of salt

FILLING
1 tablespoon butter
2 tablespoons Champion standard
　plain flour
1/2 cup brown sugar
1/2 cup sweetened condensed
　milk
1 tablespoon golden syrup
1 teaspoon vanilla essence
2 egg yolks

MERINGUE
2 egg whites
1/4 cup sugar

BASE
Cream butter and sugar, add egg and beat well. Add sifted flour, baking powder and salt. Press into a 30 cm x 20 cm sponge roll tin lined on the base with baking paper. Bake 10 to 15 minutes at 190°C. Spread cold filling over base. Top with meringue. Bake at 160°C for 20 to 25 minutes. Cut while hot.

FILLING
In a saucepan melt butter. Add flour and cook until frothy. Stir in sugar, condensed milk, golden syrup, vanilla and egg yolks. Stir continuously over a medium heat for 1 minute. Cool.

MERINGUE
Beat egg whites until stiff. Add sugar and continue beating until stiff and glossy.

CARAMEL SLICE

150 g butter
1 tablespoon golden syrup
½ cup brown sugar
1 cup Champion standard
  plain flour
1 teaspoon Edmonds
  baking powder
1 cup Fleming's rolled oats

CARAMEL ICING
1 cup brown sugar
2 tablespoons condensed milk
2 tablespoons butter
1 cup icing sugar
1 tablespoon hot water

Chocolate Icing

Melt butter, golden syrup and brown sugar in a saucepan large enough to mix all the ingredients. Mix in flour, baking powder and rolled oats until combined. Press into a shallow 20 cm square tin lined on the base with baking paper. Bake at 180°C for 15 minutes. Spread with warm caramel icing and top with chocolate icing (p. 168). Cut into squares or fingers.
(Pictured below left.)

CARAMEL ICING
Combine brown sugar, condensed milk and butter in a saucepan. Heat until bubbling and remove from heat. Add icing sugar and water. Beat to combine.

CHINESE CHEWS

2 eggs
1 cup brown sugar
75 g butter, melted
1 teaspoon vanilla essence
1½ cups Champion standard
  plain flour

1 teaspoon Edmonds
  baking powder
pinch of salt
½ cup Fleming's rolled oats
¾ cup chopped dates
¾ cup chopped walnuts
¾ cup crystallised ginger

Beat eggs and sugar until well mixed. Add butter and vanilla. Into a large bowl sift flour, baking powder and salt. Stir in rolled oats. Pour egg mixture into the sifted dry ingredients. Add dates, walnuts and ginger. Mix well. Spread mixture into a 23 cm square cake tin lined on the base with baking paper. Bake at 180°C for 30 to 35 minutes or until cooked. Cut into squares while still hot.

CHOCOLATE BROWNIE

175 g butter
250 g cooking chocolate
1½ cups Champion standard
    plain flour
1 cup sugar

2 teaspoons vanilla essence
3 eggs, beaten
icing sugar
Chocolate Icing
1 cup walnuts, chopped (optional)

In a medium-sized saucepan, melt butter and chocolate over a low heat. Remove saucepan from the heat and add flour, sugar, vanilla and eggs. Stir until well combined. Pour mixture into a 20 cm square tin lined on the base with baking paper. Bake at 180°C for 40 minutes. Leave in tin for 10 minutes before turning out onto a wire rack. When cold, sprinkle with icing sugar, or ice with chocolate icing (p. 168) and top with chopped walnuts. Cut into squares.

COCONUT DREAM

125 g butter, softened
1/2 cup brown sugar
1 1/2 cups Champion standard
  plain flour
1 teaspoon Edmonds
  baking powder

4 teaspoons Champion standard
  plain flour
1/2 teaspoon Edmonds baking
  powder
1 teaspoon vanilla essence
1 1/2 cups coconut
1 cup chopped nuts

TOPPING
2 eggs
1 cup brown sugar

Cream butter and sugar until light and fluffy. Sift flour and baking powder together. Mix into creamed mixture. Press into a 20 x 30 cm sponge roll tin lined on the base with baking paper. Bake at 200°C for 8 minutes. Pour topping mixture over cooked base. Bake at 160°C for 40 to 45 minutes or until brown. Cut into squares. *(Pictured below left.)*

TOPPING
Beat eggs. Add sugar and beat until thick. Sift flour and baking powder together. Fold into egg mixture. Stir in vanilla, coconut and nuts.

DATE SHORTCAKE

1 1/2 cups chopped dates
2 tablespoons water
3 tablespoons lemon juice
125 g butter, softened
1/2 cup sugar
1 egg

1 cup Champion standard
  plain flour
1 cup Edmonds Fielder's cornflour
1 teaspoon Edmonds
  baking powder
Lemon Icing

Put dates into a small saucepan, add water and lemon juice. Cook over a low heat until dates are soft. Cool. In a bowl cream butter and sugar until light and fluffy. Add egg, then sifted flour, cornflour and baking powder. Knead. Roll out half the mixture and place on a cold greased tray. Spread date mixture on shortcake. Roll out other half of shortcake and place on top. Bake at 190°C for 25 minutes. When cold, ice with lemon icing (p. 168). Cut into squares.

FRUIT SQUARES

200 g packet flaky pastry
icing sugar

FRUIT FILLING
50 g butter, melted
1 medium Granny Smith apple,
    peeled, cored and grated
1/4 cup raisins
1/4 cup sultanas
1/4 cup currants
1 tablespoon lemon juice
1/4 teaspoon grated lemon rind
1 teaspoon cinnamon
1/4 cup brown sugar
1 teaspoon mixed spice

Divide pastry in two. On a lightly floured board roll out one half to 2 mm thickness, forming a large rectangle approximately 20 x 30 cm. Spread fruit filling over pastry, leaving a 1 cm border around the edge for sealing. Moisten the edges with water. Roll out remaining pastry to the same thickness and shape. Place on top of fruit filling. Press edges together. Prick pastry top with a fork. Bake at 200°C for 30 to 35 minutes or until golden. Cut while hot and sprinkle with sifted icing sugar.

FRUIT FILLING
In a bowl combine all ingredients.

GINGER CRUNCH

125 g butter, softened
1/2 cup sugar
1 1/2 cups Champion standard
    plain flour
1 teaspoon Edmonds
    baking powder
1 teaspoon ground ginger

GINGER ICING
75 g butter
3/4 cup icing sugar
2 tablespoons golden syrup
3 teaspoons ground ginger

Cream butter and sugar until light and fluffy. Sift flour, baking powder and ginger together. Mix into creamed mixture. Turn dough out onto a lightly floured board. Knead well. Press dough into a 20 x 30 cm sponge roll tin lined on the base with baking paper. Bake at 190°C for 20 to 25 minutes or until light brown. Pour hot ginger icing over base. Cut into squares while still warm.

GINGER ICING
In a small saucepan combine butter, icing sugar, golden syrup and ginger. Heat until butter is melted, stirring constantly.

LEMON SLICE

150 g butter
1 cup Champion standard
    plain flour
1/2 cup icing sugar

TOPPING
2 tablespoons Edmonds
    custard powder
1/2 teaspoon Edmonds
    baking powder
1 cup sugar
1/2 cup lemon juice
1 tablespoon grated lemon rind
3 eggs

Melt the butter. Remove from heat and mix in flour and icing sugar. Press into the base of a 20 x 30 cm sponge roll tin lined with baking paper. Bake at 180°C for 15 to 20 minutes or until lightly golden. Pour over topping and bake for a further 25 minutes or until set. Cut into slices when cold.

TOPPING
Mix custard powder, baking powder, sugar, lemon juice, lemon rind and eggs together until combined.

LOUISE CAKE

150 g butter, softened
1/4 cup sugar
4 eggs, separated
2 1/2 cups Champion standard
    plain flour
2 teaspoons Edmonds
    baking powder
1/4 cup raspberry jam
1/2 cup sugar
1/2 cup coconut

Cream butter and first measure of sugar until light and fluffy. Beat in egg yolks. Sift flour and baking powder together. Stir into creamed mixture. Press dough into a 20 x 30 cm sponge roll tin lined on the base with baking paper. Spread raspberry jam over the base. In a bowl beat egg whites until stiff but not dry. Mix in the second measure of sugar and coconut. Spread this meringue mixture over jam. Bake at 180°C for 30 minutes or until meringue is dry and lightly coloured. Cut into squares while still warm.

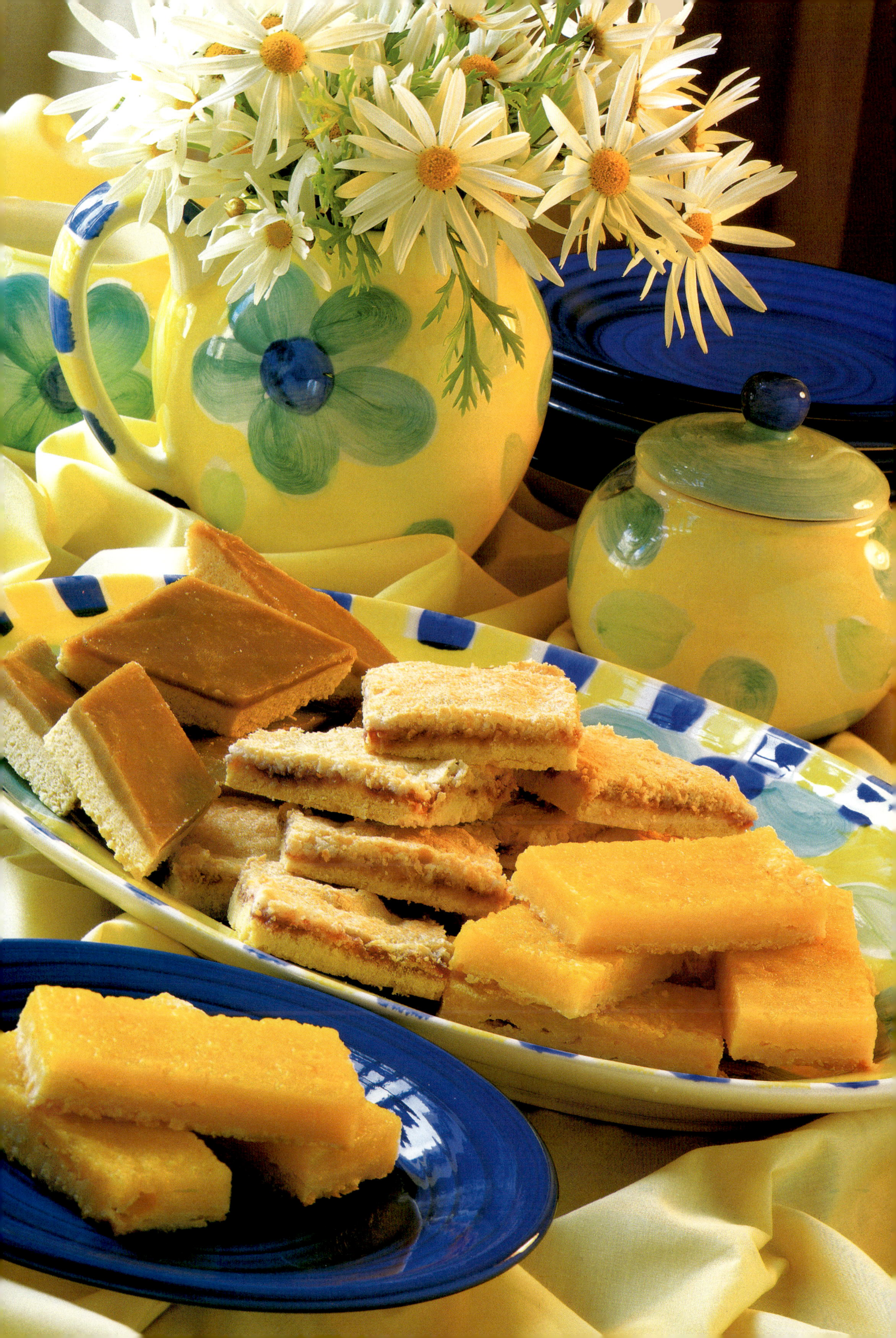

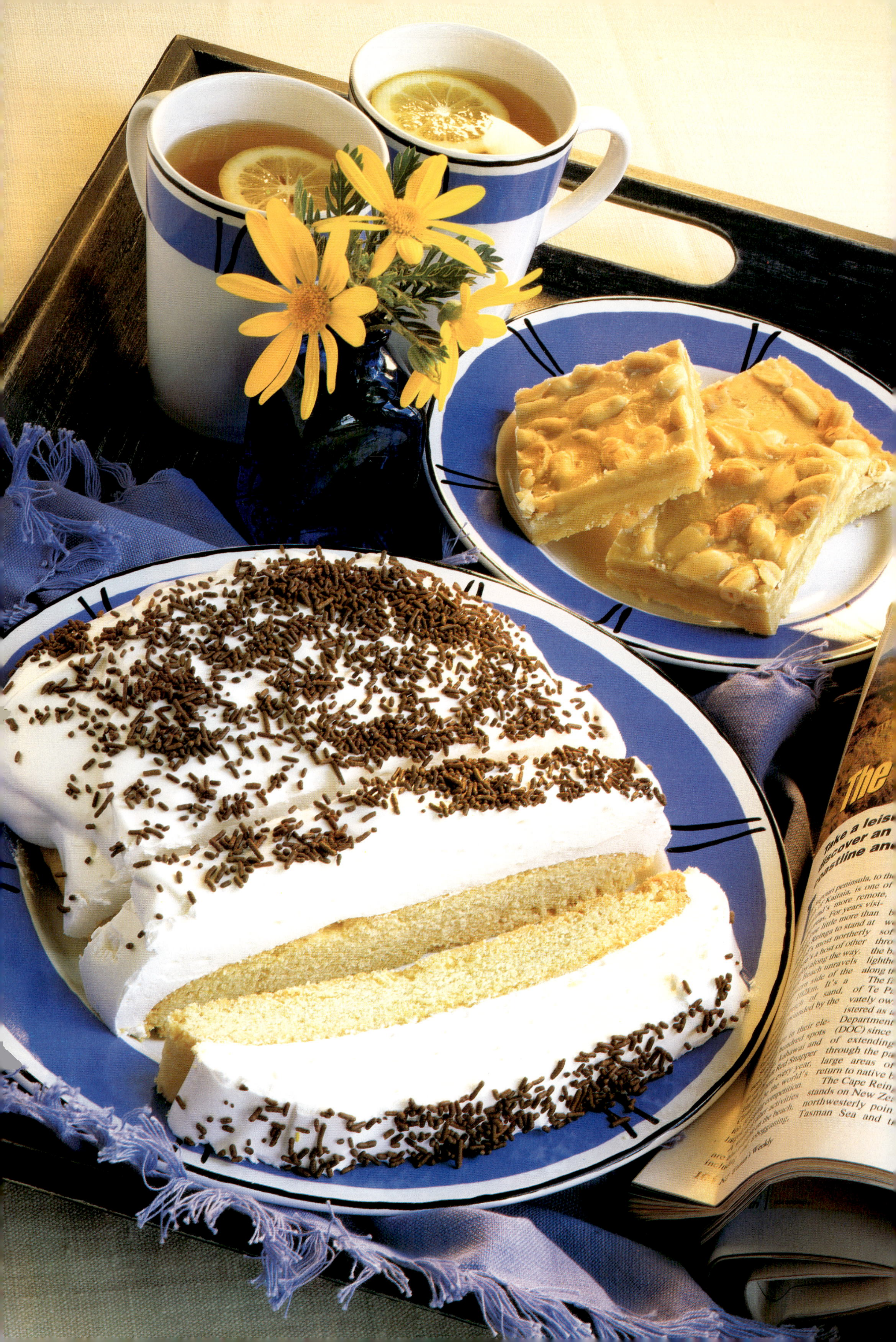

MARSHMALLOW SHORTCAKE

125 g butter, softened
1/2 cup sugar
1/2 teaspoon vanilla essence
1 egg
1 3/4 cups Champion standard
    plain flour
1 teaspoon Edmonds
    baking powder
chocolate hail or coconut

TOPPING
2 tablespoons gelatine
1 cup cold water
1 cup sugar
1 egg white
1 cup icing sugar

Cream butter and sugar, add essence. Add egg, then sifted flour and baking powder. Mix until well combined. Press in a 20 x 30 cm sponge roll tin lined on the base with baking paper and bake at 180°C for 30 minutes. Spread topping on shortcake immediately. Sprinkle with chocolate hail or coconut.

TOPPING
Soften gelatine in cold water, add sugar and boil for 8 minutes. Cool. Beat egg white until stiff and fold in icing sugar. Slowly pour in cooled gelatine. Beat until white and thick.

Variation: Soak 1 packet of Lemon or Raspberry Jelly Crystals in 1 1/2 cups cold water for 10 minutes and boil exactly 8 minutes without stirring. Leave until slightly cool. Add 1 cup icing sugar and beat until stiff. Spread on shortcake mixture and sprinkle with coconut or ice with chocolate icing (p. 168) and sprinkle with chopped walnuts.

PEANUT SHORTCAKE

250 g butter
1 teaspoon vanilla essence
1 cup sugar
2 1/4 cups Champion standard
    plain flour
2 teaspoons Edmonds baking powder

TOPPING
100 g butter
2 tablespoons golden syrup
1 cup icing sugar
1 cup roasted peanuts

Melt butter in a saucepan large enough to mix all the ingredients. Remove from heat and stir in vanilla and sugar. Sift in flour and baking powder and mix until combined. Press into a 20 x 30 cm sponge roll tin lined on the base with baking paper. Bake at 180°C for 20 minutes or until lightly golden. Spread with topping. Cut into squares.

TOPPING
Melt butter and golden syrup in a saucepan. Mix in icing sugar and peanuts until combined.

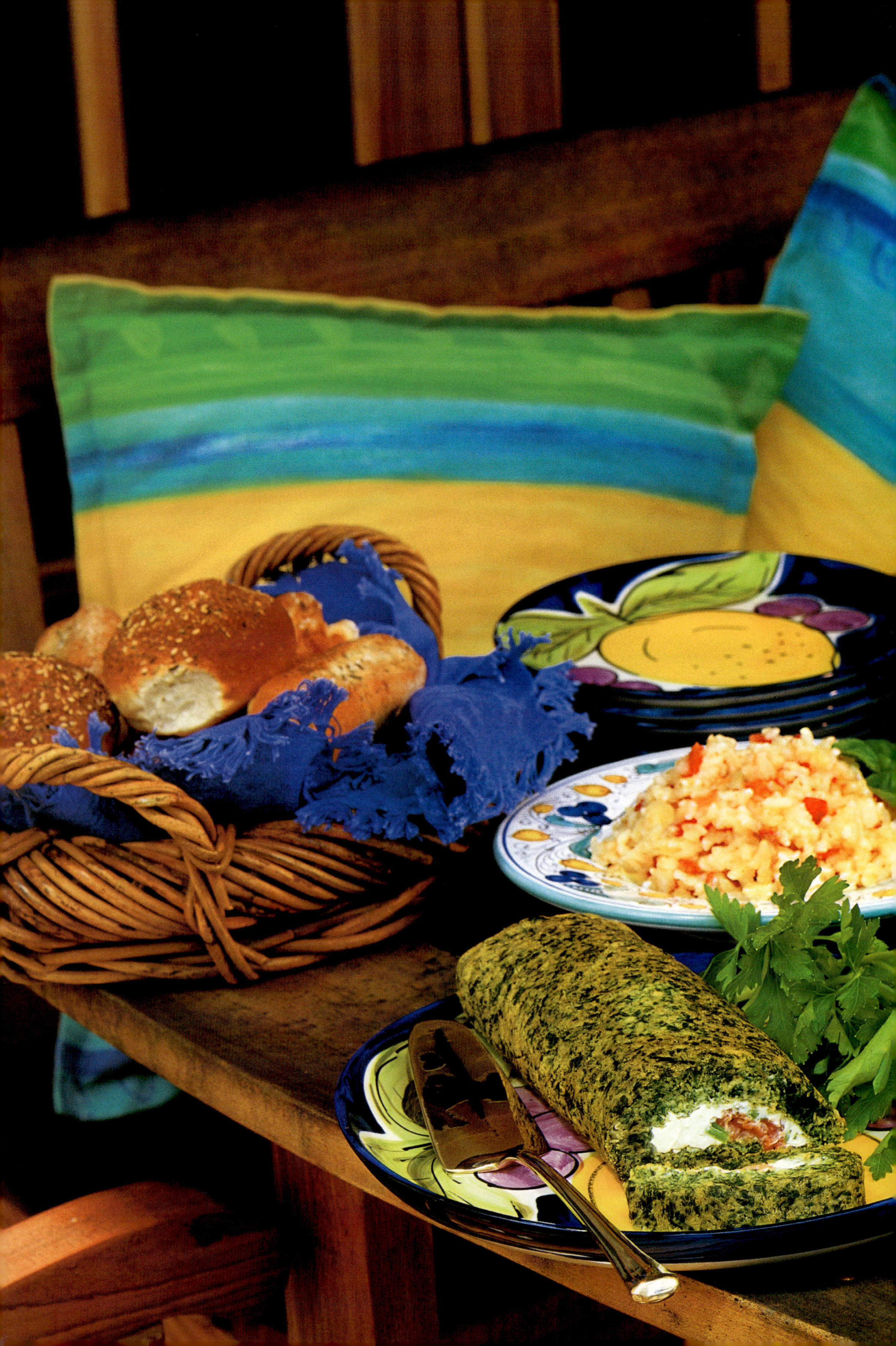

LIGHT MEALS

NIBBLES

ANTIPASTO

425 g can artichoke hearts
1/2 cup black olives
6 to 8 slices smoked beef or pork

250 g tasty cheese
cherry tomatoes
6 to 8 slices salami

Rinse artichoke hearts. Drain. Arrange artichokes, olives, beef, cheese, tomatoes and salami decoratively on a serving platter. *Serves 4 – 6.* *(Pictured left.)*

CROSTINI

2 cloves garlic
1/4 cup olive oil
1 loaf French bread

Crush, peel and mash garlic. Mix with oil. Cut bread into 1 cm slices. Brush bread liberally with garlic-flavoured oil. Place on a baking tray and bake at 190°C for 10 minutes. Turn and cook the other side for 2 to 3 minutes. Leave until cold and use as wished or store in an airtight container. *Makes about 60.* *(Pictured below left.)*

GUACAMOLE (AVOCADO DIP)

1 ripe avocado
1/2 cup sour cream
2 teaspoons lemon juice

few drops Tabasco sauce
1/4 to 1/2 teaspoon chilli powder
salt

Remove flesh from avocado and mash. Mix in sour cream, lemon juice, Tabasco sauce and chilli powder. Season with salt to taste. Cover. Chill until ready to serve. *Makes about 1 cup.*

HUMMUS (CHICK PEA DIP)

1 cup chick peas
1 onion, finely chopped
3 tablespoons tahini

1 teaspoon ground cumin
¼ cup oil
2 tablespoons lemon juice

Put the chick peas into a bowl. Cover with boiling water. Stand for 1 hour. Drain. Cook in boiling, salted water for 1 hour or until tender. Drain and allow to cool. Put chick peas into a food processor or blender. Add onion, tahini, cumin, oil and lemon juice. Process until smooth. Chill until ready to serve. **Makes about 1½ cups.** *(Pictured right.)*

BACON-WRAPPED BANANAS

2 bananas
lemon juice
4 rashers bacon

Peel bananas and cut each into 4 pieces. Brush with lemon juice. Cut each rasher of bacon in half. Wrap bananas in bacon. Secure with toothpicks. Grill on both sides until bacon is cooked. Serve warm. **Makes 8.**

DEVILS ON HORSEBACK

8 well-soaked or cooked prunes
4 rashers bacon

Remove stone from prunes. Cut each rasher of bacon in half. Wrap each prune in bacon. Secure with a toothpick. Place on an oven tray. Grill on both sides until bacon is cooked. Serve warm. **Makes 8.**

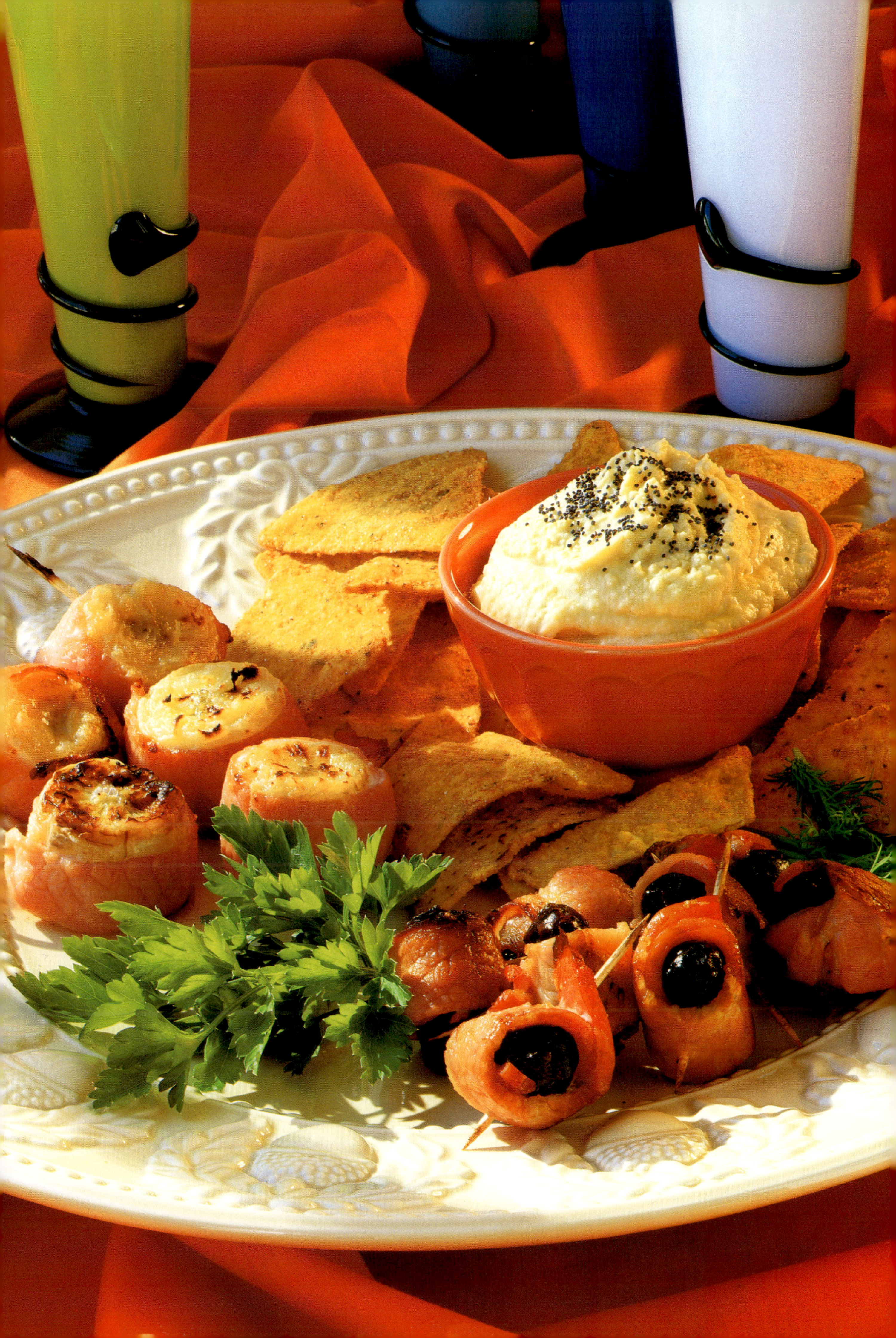

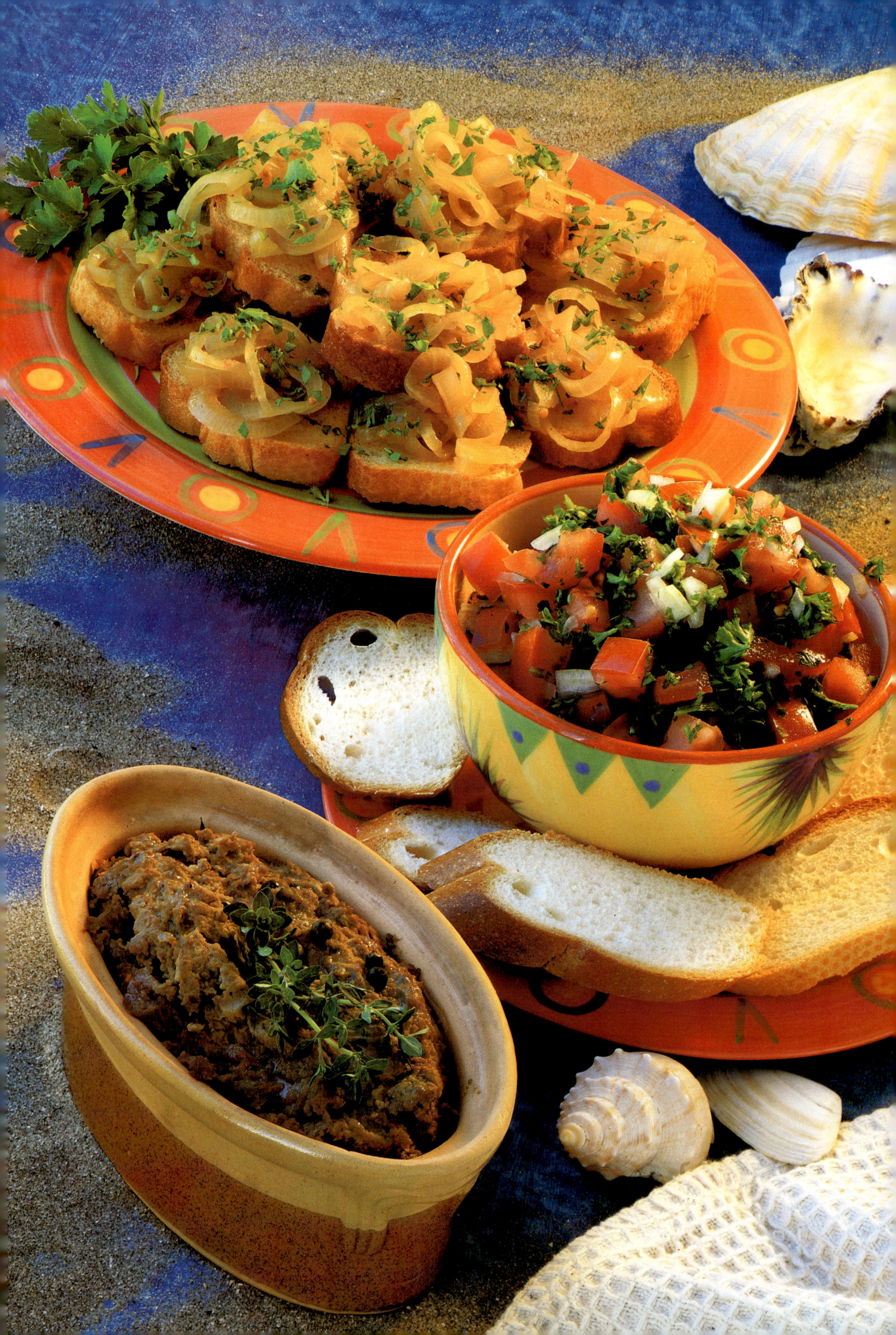

CHICKEN LIVER PATÉ

1 onion
1 clove garlic
50 g butter
350 g chicken livers
2 teaspoons prepared French
   mustard

2 tablespoons sherry
1/4 teaspoon salt
1 tablespoon drained green
   peppercorns
Coarsely ground black pepper
Fresh herbs

Peel onion and chop roughly. Crush, peel and chop garlic. Melt butter in a frying pan and sauté onion and garlic for 5 minutes or until clear. Place in a blender or food processor. Remove any fat or gristle from chicken livers. Chop livers and add to onion pan. Sauté until they lose their pinkness. Add to onion in blender with mustard, sherry and salt. Blend until smooth. Mix in peppercorns and pack into a serving dish. Coarsely grind black pepper over and garnish with fresh herbs. **Makes about 2 cups.** *(Main picture, bottom left.)*

ONION MARMALADE

4 medium onions
1/2 cup water
1/4 cup brown sugar

1/2 cup DYC spiced vinegar
1 tablespoon mustard seeds

Peel onions and slice finely. Place in a saucepan with water, brown sugar, spiced vinegar and mustard seeds. Cook over a moderate heat for about 20 minutes or until liquid has evaporated. Serve as a topping for crostini, in pita bread, as a meat accompaniment or on open sandwiches. **Makes about 1 cup.** *(Pictured top left.)*

TOMATO SALSA

1 large tomato, chopped
1/4 cup chopped fresh coriander or
   parsley
2 tablespoons finely chopped onion
1 tablespoon lime or lemon juice

Combine all ingredients in a bowl. Set aside for 1 hour before serving. **Makes 1 1/2 cups.**

BREAKFASTS

BACON RASHERS

bacon

Cut rind and fat from bacon using scissors. Cut rashers in half if long. Rub bacon fat over the base of a frying pan. Arrange bacon in a single layer over base of heated pan. Cook over a moderate heat for 4 minutes for regular bacon or 5 minutes for crisp bacon. Drain on absorbent paper. **Serves 4.** *(Pictured below left.)*

BANANAS WITH MAPLE SYRUP

4 bananas
1/2 cup maple syrup

Wash and dry unpeeled bananas. Place bananas in a dry frying pan and cook over a moderate heat for about 5 minutes, turning during cooking. Cut bananas lengthwise and partly peel back skin. Spoon over 1 tablespoon of maple syrup into each split banana. Serve with bacon and eggs. **Serves 4.** *(Main picture.)*

BREAKFAST MUSHROOMS

100 g brown button mushrooms
1 clove garlic
25 g butter
2 teaspoons Edmonds Fielder's cornflour
1 cup low-fat milk
1 tablespoon chopped parsley
3 slices wholemeal toast

Wipe mushrooms and cut in half if large. Crush, peel and finely chop garlic. Melt butter in a saucepan. Sauté garlic and mushrooms for 3 minutes. Mix cornflour to a paste with a little of the measured milk. Add remaining milk to mushrooms. Bring to the boil and stir in the cornflour paste. Stir until mixture boils and thickens. Mix in parsley. Cut toast in half diagonally. Trim crusts if wished. Allow three toast triangles per serving. Spoon mushroom mixture over toast. Serve hot. **Serves 2.** *(Pictured above right.)*

EGGS BENEDICT

3 English muffins
1 tablespoon butter
6 slices ham
6 eggs
salt
pepper
1/2 cup Hollandaise sauce

Split the muffins and toast. Keep warm. Melt the butter in a frying pan. Add ham and cook until golden on both sides. While ham is cooking, poach the eggs. Place a slice of ham on each muffin. Place poached eggs on top of ham. Season with salt and pepper to taste. Top with Hollandaise sauce. *Serves 6.*

HOLLANDAISE SAUCE

50 g butter
1 tablespoon lemon juice
2 egg yolks
1/4 cup cream
1/2 teaspoon dry mustard
1/4 teaspoon salt

Melt the butter in a double boiler. Add lemon juice, egg yolks and cream. Cook, stirring constantly until thick and smooth. Do not boil or sauce will curdle. Remove from heat. Add mustard and salt and beat until smooth. **Makes 3/4 cup.** *(Pictured below left.)*

FRENCH TOAST

2 eggs
2 tablespoons milk
salt
pepper
4 to 6 slices toast bread
butter

Lightly beat eggs and milk together. Season with salt and pepper to taste. Cut slices of bread in half. Heat butter in a frying pan. Dip bread in egg. Place in frying pan and cook until golden on underside. Turn and cook the other side. Omit salt and pepper for sweet French toast. *Serves 4.*

SCRAMBLED EGG

1 egg
1 tablespoon milk
salt
pepper

1 teaspoon butter
chopped parsley
1 slice buttered toast

Lightly beat egg. Add milk, salt and pepper to taste. Melt butter in a small frying pan. Pour in egg mixture and cook over a low heat until set. Using a wooden spoon, carefully drag the mixture around the outside of the pan to the centre to allow the mixture to cook evenly. Scrambled eggs should have large clots of cooked egg so do not stir vigorously. Stir in parsley and serve on hot buttered toast. If eggs are overcooked they will become tough with a watery liquid separating out. *Serves 1. (Pictured below left.)*

VARIATIONS
Finely sliced mushrooms added into uncooked egg mixture.
Fold cooked chopped bacon in after eggs are cooked.
Fold chopped smoked salmon in after eggs are cooked.

TOASTED MUESLI

1/4 cup oil
1/4 cup brown sugar
1/4 cup honey
3 cups Fleming's rolled oats
1/2 cup coconut
1/2 cup wheatgerm

1/2 cup Fleming's bran flakes
1/2 cup sesame seeds
1/2 cup sunflower seeds
1/2 cup chopped nuts
1/2 to 1 cup raisins or sultanas

Put oil, sugar and honey into a saucepan. Heat gently until sugar dissolves. In a bowl combine rolled oats, coconut, wheatgerm, bran flakes, sesame and sunflower seeds and nuts. Pour oil mixture over and mix thoroughly. Turn into a large roasting pan. Bake at 160°C for 40 to 50 minutes or until lightly browned. Stir occasionally. Leave to cool. Add raisins or sultanas. Store in an airtight container. *Makes about 6 cups.*

LIGHT MEALS

BACON AND EGG PIE

2 sheets pre-rolled flaky pastry
1 onion, chopped
1 cup chopped bacon
½ cup mixed vegetables
2 tablespoons spicy chutney
6 eggs
milk

Use 1 sheet of pastry to line a 20 cm square shallow cake tin. Sprinkle onion, bacon and mixed vegetables evenly over pastry. Dot the chutney on top. Break eggs evenly over, piercing the yolks so they run slightly. Carefully lift second sheet of pastry over filling. Brush top with milk. Bake at 200°C for 40 minutes or until well risen and golden. To serve cut into squares. Serve hot or cold. **Serves 6.**

HASH BROWN POTATOES

500 g old potatoes, peeled and chopped
50 g butter
2 rashers bacon, finely chopped
1 tablespoon chopped chives

Cook potatoes in boiling salted water until tender. Drain well then leave to cool. Mash. Melt butter in a large frying pan. Add bacon and cook until crisp. Using a slotted spoon, remove bacon from pan. Do not discard fat. Spread potato over base of frying pan. Press down until even. Cook over a low heat for 25 minutes or until underside is deep golden brown. Turn, using a spatula, and cook other side. Scoop potato out of pan and into heated serving dish. Sprinkle with bacon and chives. *(Pictured left.)*

FRITTATA

50 g butter
2 onions, chopped
3 cups grated vegetables, e.g. courgettes, carrots, potatoes
4 eggs
2 tablespoons water
½ cup grated tasty cheese
salt
pepper
¼ cup grated Parmesan cheese

Melt butter in a large heavy-based frying pan. Add onions and cook until clear. Add vegetables and cook, stirring, for 10 minutes or until just tender. In a bowl beat together eggs, water, cheese and salt and pepper to taste. Pour this over vegetable mixture. Gently cook until egg mixture is set. Sprinkle with Parmesan. Grill until golden. To serve, cut into wedges. **Serves 4 – 6.** *(Pictured top left.)*

FRENCH ONION SOUP

3 tablespoons butter
6 medium onions, thinly sliced
1 teaspoon sugar
4 cups beef stock

salt
black pepper
¼ cup dry sherry
4 to 6 slices cheese on toast

Melt butter in a saucepan. Add onions and sugar. Cook slowly for 20 minutes or until onions are golden. Add beef stock. Bring to the boil then cover and simmer for 15 minutes. Season with salt and pepper to taste. Just before serving add sherry. Grill cheese on toast. Cut into triangles or squares and place on soup. *Serves 4 – 6.* *(Pictured below left.)*

PUMPKIN SOUP

750 g pumpkin, peeled and
    chopped
1 large potato, chopped
1 onion, chopped

4 cups chicken stock
salt
black pepper
nutmeg

Put pumpkin, potato and onion into a large saucepan. Add stock. Cover, bring to the boil and cook until vegetables are soft. Purée vegetable mixture in a blender or push through a sieve. Season with salt, pepper and nutmeg to taste. For extra flavour, a ham hock or bacon bones can be added when cooking the pumpkin. *Serves 6.*

SEAFOOD SOUP

4 cups chicken stock
few sprigs parsley
1 bay leaf
6 black peppercorns
2 tablespoons butter
2 leeks, thinly sliced
3 carrots, thinly sliced

1 turnip, thinly sliced
2 stalks celery, thinly sliced
500 g white fish fillets, cut into
    large chunks
salt
white pepper

Bring stock, parsley, bay leaf and peppercorns to the boil and simmer for 10 minutes. While stock is simmering, melt butter in another saucepan. Add leeks, carrots, turnip and celery. Gently cook without colouring until vegetables are glossy and just tender. Place fish on top of vegetables. Pour stock through a sieve onto fish and vegetables. Reheat and season with salt and pepper to taste. *Serves 6.* *(Pictured below left.)*

SPICY LENTIL SOUP

2 teaspoons butter
2 teaspoons oil
1 clove garlic, crushed
1 carrot, finely chopped
1 onion, finely chopped
1 stalk celery, finely chopped
1 teaspoon curry powder
1 cup brown lentils

250 g bacon bones
400 g can tomatoes in juice,
    chopped
4 cups beef stock
salt
black pepper
2 tablespoons chopped parsley

Heat butter and oil in a large saucepan. Add garlic, carrot, onion and celery. Cook until onion is clear. Stir in curry powder. Cook, stirring constantly, for 30 seconds. Add lentils, bacon bones, tomatoes and juice and stock. Cover. Bring to the boil, then reduce heat and simmer covered for 1½ hours or until lentils are cooked. Remove and discard bacon bones. Season with salt and pepper to taste. Serve garnished with parsley. *Serves 4 – 5.*

TUSCAN TOMATO SOUP

2 onions
2 cloves garlic
2 sticks celery
2 courgettes
2 carrots
1 tablespoon olive oil

425 g can tomatoes in juice
410 g can tomato purée
2 cups beef stock
300 g can white beans
1 teaspoon dried basil

Peel onions and chop very finely. Crush, peel and chop garlic. Trim celery and courgettes. Peel carrots. Chop celery, courgettes and carrots very finely. Heat oil in a large saucepan and sauté onion and vegetables for 5 minutes or until onion is clear. Add tomatoes in juice, tomato purée and stock. Cover and bring to the boil. Simmer for 15 minutes. Add drained beans and basil to soup and cook for a further 5 minutes. Serve hot. **Serves 4.**

BACON AND TOMATO RISOTTO

4 rashers bacon, rind removed
2 onions
50 g butter
2 cups arborio rice

6 cups chicken stock
6 tomatoes
1/4 cup torn fresh basil leaves
Grated parmesan or tasty cheese

Cut bacon into small pieces. Peel onion and chop finely. Melt butter in a risotto pan or wide deep frying pan. Sauté onion and bacon for 5 minutes or until clear. Add rice and cook for 20 minutes or until rice looks white. Add two cups of stock and cook stirring uncovered, adding more stock as liquid is absorbed. Continue cooking rice for 15 to 20 minutes, adding more stock as necessary, until rice is firm to the bite but creamy. Cut tomatoes into 1 cm cubes, removing stem end. Mix through risotto with basil. Cook for 1 minute. Sprinkle over cheese. *Serves 4 – 6.*
(Pictured below left.)

QUICHE LORRAINE

200 g short pasty
4 eggs
1 cup milk
salt

freshly ground black pepper
4 rashers bacon, rind removed
6 spring onions

Roll pastry out on a lightly floured board and use to line a 20 cm quiche dish. Bake blind at 200°C for 10 minutes. Remove baking blind material and return to oven for 3 minutes. Lightly beat eggs. Add milk, salt and pepper and beat to just combine. Cut bacon into strips. Trim spring onions and cut into quarters lengthwise. Sprinkle bacon over pastry base. Pour egg mixture through a sieve into pastry shell. Arrange spring onions over top of egg mixture. Bake at 200°C for 10 minutes, then reduce heat to 150°C and cook for a further 20 minutes or until quiche is set. Serve hot or cold. *Serves 4.*

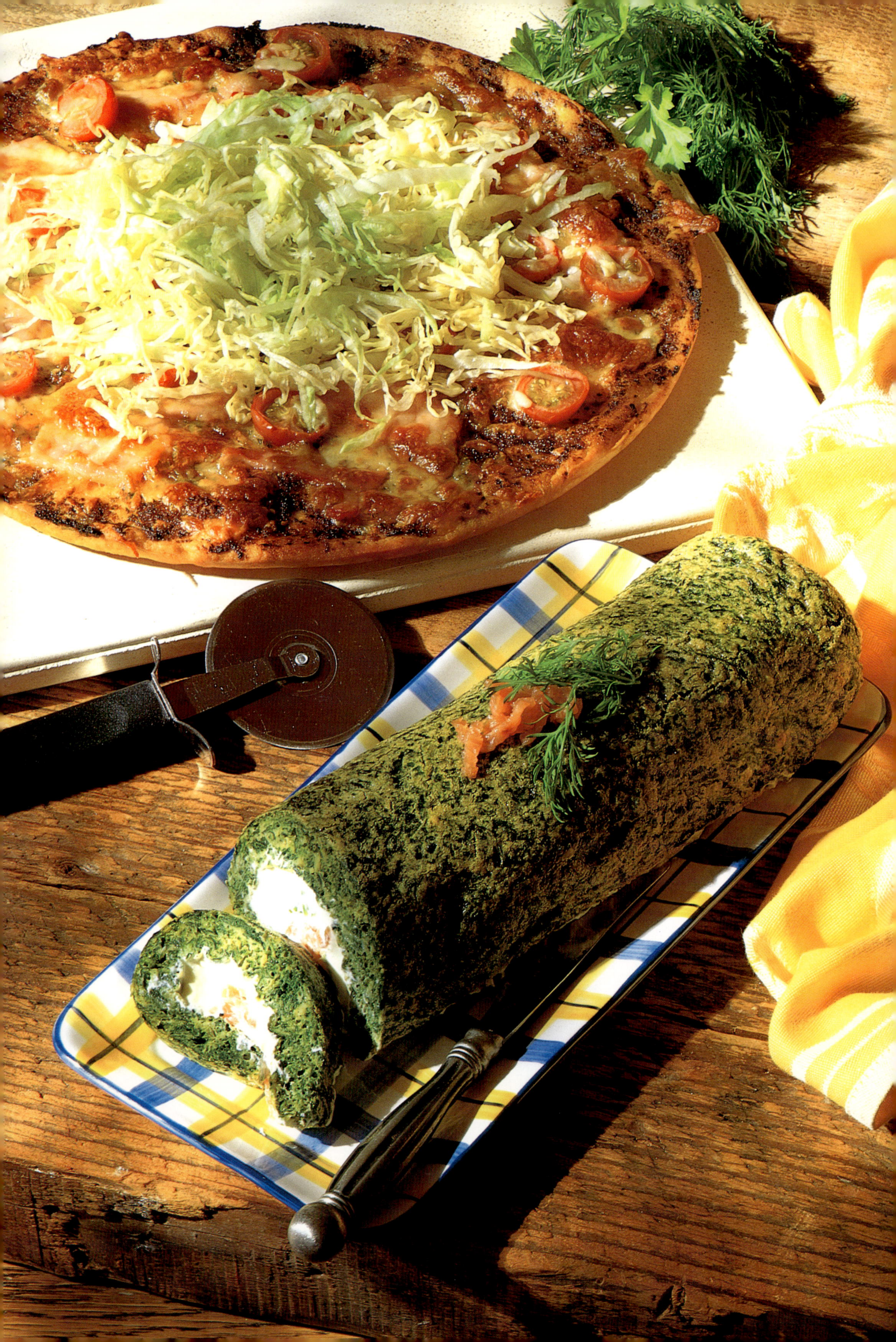

RAJAH'S PIZZA

TOPPING	PIZZA DOUGH
1/2 cup fruit chutney	1/2 teaspoon sugar
200 g cooked chicken tenderloins	1/2 cup tepid water
1/2 cup natural unsweetened yoghurt	2 teaspoons Edmonds active dry yeast
1/2 cup chopped cucumber	1 to 1 1/4 cups Champion high grade flour
1 tablespoon chopped fresh coriander or parsley	1/2 teaspoon salt
	1 tablespoon olive oil

Spread uncooked pizza base with chutney. Pile on chicken. Cook as above. Mix yoghurt and cucumber together. Spoon over cooked pizza and sprinkle with coriander or parsley.

PIZZA DOUGH

Dissolve sugar in water. Sprinkle over yeast and leave for 10 minutes or until frothy. Place 1 cup of flour and salt in a bowl. Mix in yeast mixture and olive oil to form a stiff dough. Add more flour if necessary. Knead dough until smooth and elastic. Place in a greased bowl. Turn dough over and cover with plastic wrap. Set aside in a warm place until double in bulk. Punch dough down and knead until smooth. Shape and flatten into a 30 cm round. Top with topping of your choice. Bake at 200°C for 15 minutes or until cooked. *Serves 4.*

BLT PIZZA

- 1/4 cup sundried tomato pesto
- 6 rashers bacon, rind removed
- 4 tomatoes
- 1 cup grated mozzarella cheese
- 1 cup shredded lettuce

Spread uncooked pizza base with pesto. Cut bacon into large pieces. Arrange on pizza base. Chop tomatoes roughly and pile on bacon. Top with cheese. Cook as above. Pile lettuce on top.
(Pictured top left.)

SPINACH AND SMOKED SALMON ROULADE

- 450 g packet frozen spinach
- 4 eggs
- 1/4 teaspoon salt
- 1/2 cup Champion standard plain flour
- 1 teaspoon Edmonds baking powder
- 1/4 teaspoon ground nutmeg
- 25 g melted butter
- 250 g pot low-fat sour cream
- 1/4 cup chopped fresh chives
- 100 g smoked salmon slices

Thaw spinach and drain well, squeezing out as much water as possible. Beat eggs and salt until thick, creamy and they hold their shape. Sift flour, baking powder and nutmeg into egg mixture. Fold in with butter and spinach. Pour mixture into a 20 x 30 cm sponge roll tin lined with baking paper. Bake at 200°C for 15 minutes or until roulade springs back when lightly touched. Turn out onto a clean tea-towel. Remove baking paper and roll up from the long side. Leave wrapped in the tea-towel until cool. Unroll and spread with sour cream. Sprinkle over chives and arrange smoked salmon over. Reroll roulade. Serve sliced. *Serves 6.*

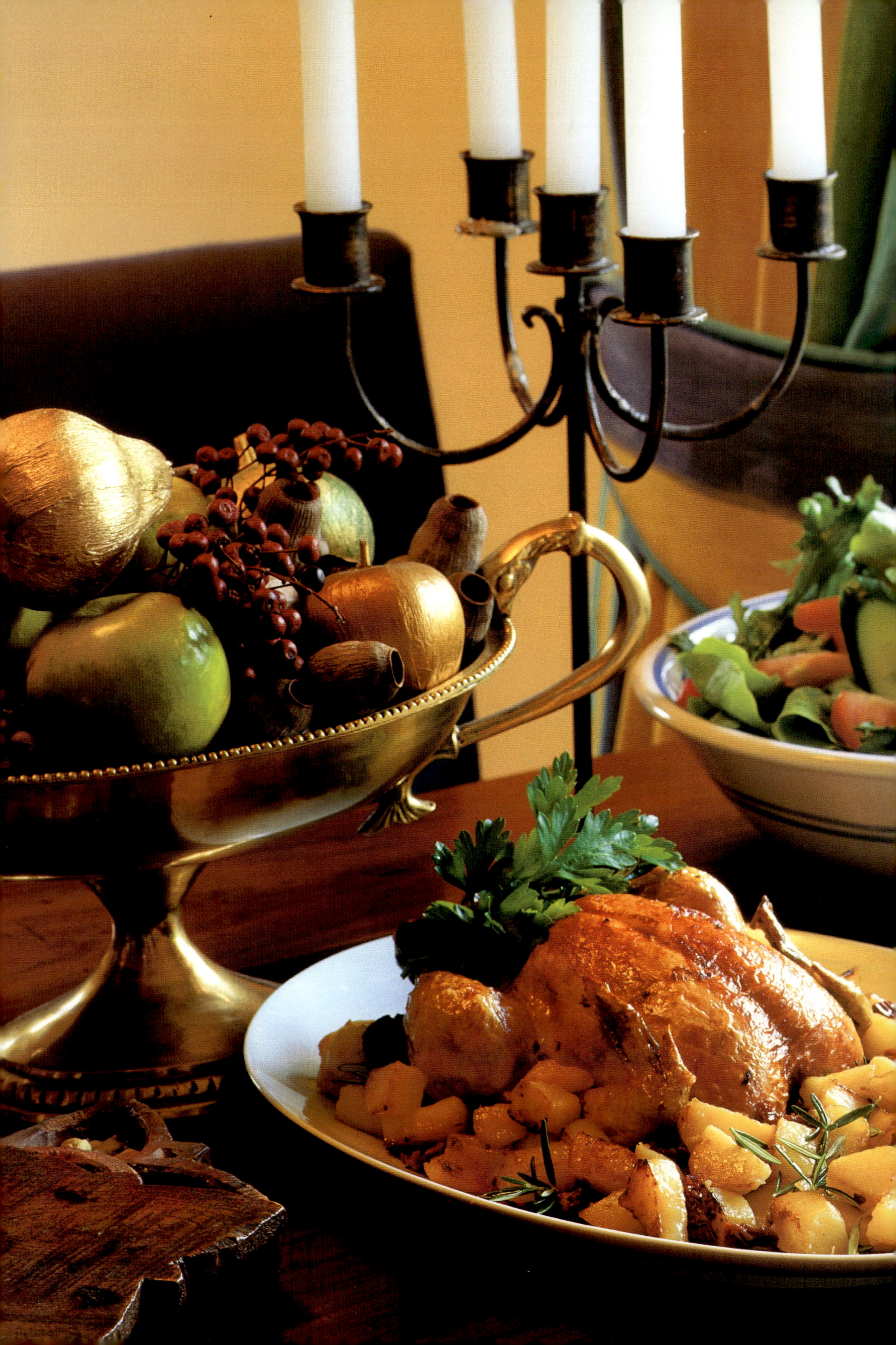

HOME-COOKED MEALS

PASTA

BOLOGNESE SAUCE

2 tablespoons oil
2 large onions, finely chopped
500 g mince
¼ cup tomato paste
400 g can tomatoes in juice
1 teaspoon basil
1 teaspoon oregano
4 cups water
salt
black pepper
500 g Diamond spaghetti, cooked
grated Parmesan cheese

Heat oil in a large frying pan. Add onion and cook until golden, stirring constantly. Stir in meat and quickly cook until browned on all sides. Add tomato paste. Push tomatoes and juice through sieve. Add to pan. Stir in basil, oregano and water. Bring to the boil, reduce heat and cook uncovered for 45 minutes or until mixture is a thick sauce consistency. Season with salt and pepper to taste. Serve over hot pasta garnished with Parmesan cheese. *Serves 4 – 6.*
(Pictured below left.)

CARBONARA
(HAM AND MUSHROOM SAUCE)

2 tablespoons oil
2 ham steaks, chopped
1 onion, chopped
200 g mushrooms, sliced
250 g pot sour cream
1 egg yolk
pepper
375 g Diamond pasta, cooked –
    e.g. seashells, fettucine
1 tablespoon chopped parsley

Heat oil in a frying pan or saucepan. Add ham and onion. Cook until onion is clear and ham slightly browned. Stir in mushrooms and cook for a further 2 minutes. Remove from heat. In a bowl beat sour cream and egg yolk together. Add this to ham mixture. Return to a low heat and cook, stirring constantly until sauce thickens slightly. Do not allow to boil. Season with pepper to taste. Add hot pasta. Stir to combine. Garnish with parsley. *Serves 4 – 6.*

FRESH TOMATO AND BASIL SAUCE

500 g ripe tomatoes
1 onion
1 clove garlic
1 tablespoon olive oil
1 teaspoon prepared minced chilli

½ cup chopped fresh basil
250 g Diamond Italian Style
  farfalle pasta, cooked
grated cheese

Blanch tomatoes in boiling water for 1 minute. Drain and plunge into cold water. Peel and remove stem end. Cut tomatoes roughly. Peel onion and chop finely. Crush, peel and chop garlic. Heat oil in a saucepan and sauté onion and garlic for 5 minutes or until onion is clear. Add chilli and sauté for 30 seconds. Add tomatoes and half the basil and cook sauce over a low heat for 15 minutes or until pulpy. Mix in remaining basil. Toss tomato and basil sauce through pasta. Garnish with grated cheese. *Serves 4.* (Main picture, bottom right.)

LASAGNE

MEAT SAUCE
2 tablespoons oil
1 onion, chopped
3 cloves garlic, crushed
500 g mince
100 g mushrooms, sliced
2 x 400 g cans tomatoes in juice,
  chopped
1 cup tomato purée
1 teaspoon oregano
½ teaspoon basil
1 teaspoon sugar
salt
pepper

CHEESE SAUCE
50 g butter
3 tablespoons Champion standard
  plain flour
1 ½ cups milk
¾ cup grated cheese
salt
pepper

300 g packet Diamond Italian
  Style wide lasagne, cooked
2 tablespoons grated Parmesan
  cheese

MEAT SAUCE
Heat oil in a large frying pan. Add onion and garlic. Cook until onion is golden. Increase heat. Add meat and brown well. Add mushrooms, tomatoes in juice, tomato purée, oregano, basil and sugar. Stir. Bring to the boil then reduce heat and simmer gently for 40 minutes or until meat mixture has thickened slightly, stirring occasionally. Season with salt and pepper to taste. Set aside until cool.

CHEESE SAUCE
Melt butter in a saucepan. Add flour and cook until frothy. Gradually add milk, stirring constantly until mixture boils and thickens. Remove from heat. Stir in cheese. Season with salt and pepper to taste. Cover with a lid or plastic wrap to prevent a skin forming. Set aside until cool.

Place half the lasagne in a greased ovenproof dish. Spread with half the meat mixture and half the cheese sauce. Repeat the layers. Top with Parmesan cheese. Cook at 180°C for 20 minutes or until golden and heated through. *Serves 4 – 6.*

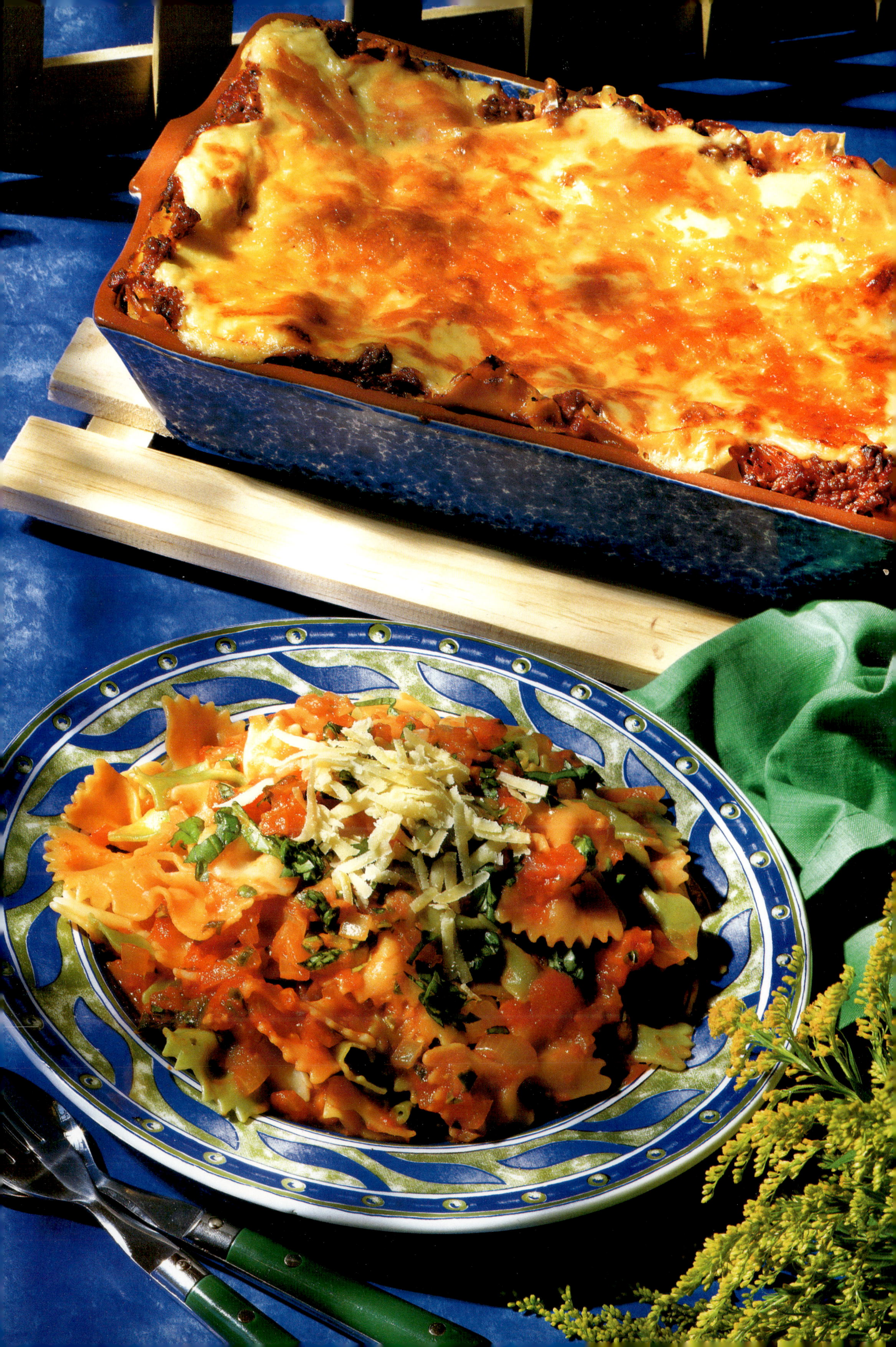

MARINARA (SEAFOOD SAUCE)

½ cup dry white wine
1 small onion, chopped
12 fresh mussels, scrubbed and debearded
250 g white fish fillets – e.g. gurnard, tarakihi, snapper
1 teaspoon oil
1 clove garlic, chopped
400 g can tomatoes in juice
¼ cup chopped parsley
100 g cooked shrimps
250 g Diamond pasta, cooked – e.g. bows, spaghetti

Put wine, onion and mussels into a large frying pan. Cover and cook until mussels open. Remove mussels from shell. Discard any which do not open. Add fish to pan and gently cook for 10 minutes or until fish flakes easily. Carefully lift fish from pan, reserving all liquid. Continue cooking until liquid has reduced by half. In a separate saucepan, heat oil and garlic and cook until golden. Stir in tomatoes in juice and parsley. Bring to the boil. Add reserved fish liquid. Mash tomatoes slightly. Reduce heat and cook uncovered until sauce thickens slightly. Stir in mussels, shrimps and fish. Gently heat through. Serve over hot pasta. *Serves 4 – 6.*

PESTO (BASIL AND GARLIC SAUCE)

1 tablespoon oil
2 tablespoons pinenuts
3 cloves garlic, chopped
2 cups fresh basil leaves

¼ cup oil
salt
black pepper
200 g Diamond spaghetti, cooked

Heat first measure of oil in a small frying pan. Add pinenuts and cook, stirring frequently until golden. Drain on absorbent paper. Put the garlic, basil and pinenuts into bowl of food processor or blender. Process until finely chopped. Continue processing while adding second measure of oil in a thin, steady stream. Process for a few seconds until just combined. Season with salt and pepper to taste. Serve over hot pasta. *Serves 4.* *(Pictured below left.)*

ROASTED PEPPER AND PUMPKIN LASAGNE

375 g Diamond lasagne
1 cup cooked mashed pumpkin
pinch ground nutmeg
1 egg

2 red peppers
250 g pot low fat sour cream
2 rashers bacon, rind removed
1 cup grated tasty cheese

Cook lasagne to packet directions. Drain. Mix pumpkin, nutmeg and egg together. Cut peppers in half lengthwise. Remove core and seeds. Grill until skins are golden and blistered. Remove from oven and peel when cool enough to handle. Chop peppers very finely or purée in a food processor or blender. Mix peppers and sour cream together. Place a layer of cooked lasagne in the bottom of an oiled lasagne or ovenproof dish. Spread with mashed pumpkin. Arrange a layer of lasagne on top and spread with pepper mixture. Repeat layers finishing with a layer of lasagne. Cut bacon into small pieces. Mix bacon and cheese together and sprinkle over lasagne. Bake at 180°C for 25 minutes or until hot and lightly golden. *Serves 4 – 6.*

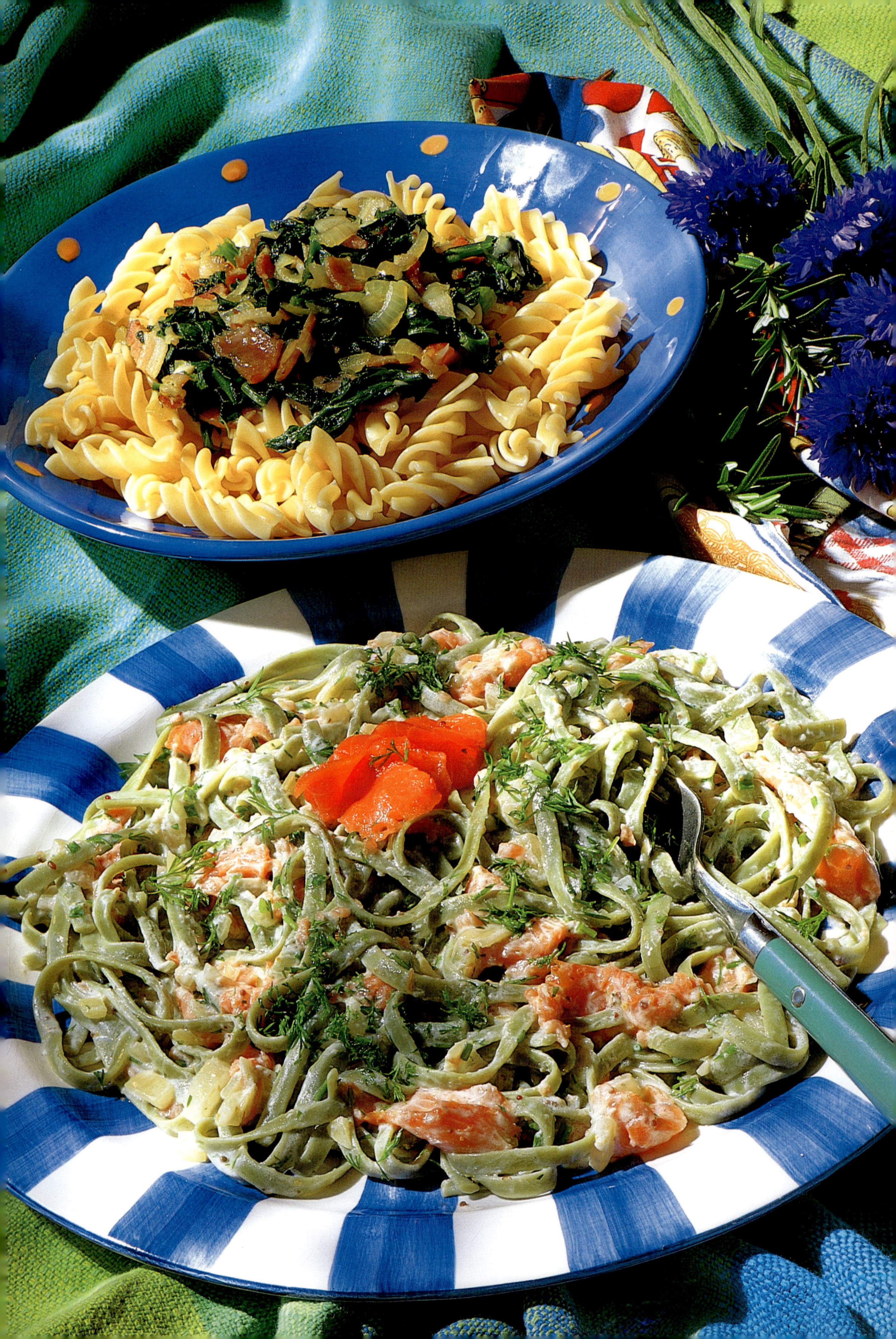

SMOKED SALMON PASTA SAUCE

200 g wood-roasted salmon
1 small onion
1 clove garlic
1 teaspoon oil
1 teaspoon prepared whole seed mustard
1 tablespoon chopped parsley

1 tablespoon chopped fresh dill
1 tablespoon chopped fresh chives
1 cup natural unsweetened yoghurt
500 g Diamond Italian Style egg fettucine

Remove skin from salmon and flake flesh. Peel onion and chop finely. Crush, peel and chop garlic. Heat oil and sauté onion and garlic for 5 minutes or until clear. Add salmon, mustard, parsley, dill, chives and yoghurt. Bring to the boil and then reduce heat. Cook pasta to packet directions. Drain. Toss through smoked salmon sauce. **Serves 4.** *(Pictured below left.)*

SPINACH AND BACON SAUCE

1 tablespoon butter
1 onion, chopped
1 clove garlic, crushed
4 rashers bacon, chopped

2–3 bunches spinach, chopped
250 g Diamond pasta, cooked – e.g. spirals, spaghetti

Melt butter in a large frying pan. Add onion, garlic and bacon. Cook until onion is clear and bacon is cooked. Stir in spinach and cook for a further 2 minutes or until spinach is a rich, dark green colour, stirring constantly. Serve over hot pasta. **Serves 4.**

SEAFOOD

FISH PIE

25 g butter
1 tablespoon milk
3 cups cooked mashed potatoes
3/4 teaspoon salt
black pepper
1 tablespoon butter
1 tablespoon Champion standard
  plain flour

1 cup milk
500 g smoked fish, flaked, or 425 g
  can tuna, drained and flaked
1 tablespoon chopped parsley
2 hard-boiled eggs, chopped

Mix first measure of butter and milk into the potatoes, beating with a fork to combine. Season with salt and pepper to taste. Line a 20 cm pie dish with half the potatoes. Set remaining potatoes aside. Heat second measure of butter in a saucepan. Stir in flour and cook until frothy. Gradually add second measure of milk, stirring constantly until sauce boils and thickens. Remove from heat. Add fish, parsley and eggs. Pour this mixture into the lined pie dish. Cover with remaining potato. Cook at 190°C for 20 minutes or until pale golden. **Serves 4 – 6.**
(Main picture, bottom left.)

CRISPY CHINESE BATTER

Edmonds Fielder's cornflour
1 egg white

Coat the items to be cooked with cornflour. Lightly beat egg white with a fork. Dip the coated items in egg white then deep-fry. Drain on absorbent paper.

STIR-FRIED LEMON AND GINGER FISH

4 medium skinned and boned fish
  fillets
1 medium onion
1 tablespoon peanut oil
1 tablespoon grated root ginger
1 tablespoon Edmonds Fielder's
  cornflour

1/4 cup lemon juice
1 teaspoon grated lemon rind
1 cup chicken stock
1 tablespoon brown sugar
chopped spring onion greens

Cut fish into 2-cm-wide strips, about 6 cm long. Peel onion and cut into eighths. Heat oil in a wok or heavy frying pan and stir-fry onion and ginger for 2 minutes. Add fish and stir-fry for 2 minutes or until fish is almost cooked. Mix cornflour and lemon juice together until smooth. Add lemon rind, stock and brown sugar. Pour over fish. Bring to the boil and cook for 1 minute. Serve garnished with spring onion greens. **Serves 4.** *(Pictured top left.)*

ITALIAN BAKED FISH

1 onion
4 medium skinned and boned
　fish fillets
400 g can tomatoes in juice
½ cup tomato purée

1 tablespoon prepared minced
　chilli
1 teaspoon dried basil
2 tablespoons capers
¼ cup pitted black olives
freshly ground black pepper

Peel onion and cut into rings. Place fish in an ovenproof dish. Arrange onion rings over fish. Roughly chop tomatoes. Mix tomatoes and juice, tomato purée, chilli, basil, capers and olives together. Pour over fish. Cover and bake at 180°C for 20 to 25 minutes or until fish is cooked. Season with freshly ground black pepper and serve hot. **Serves 4.**

MUSSEL SOUP

250 g skinned and boned fish
  fillets
4 cups water
400 g can tomatoes in juice
2 tablespoons butter
1 teaspoon curry powder
2 tablespoons Champion standard
  plain flour
¼ cup dry white wine

2 teaspoons chicken stock powder
2 tablespoons tomato paste
¼ teaspoon dried basil
16 – 20 fresh cleaned mussels in
  shell
salt
black pepper
chopped parsley

Put fish and water into a large saucepan. Bring to the boil then simmer for 15 minutes. Remove fish from pan and flake. Reserve all the liquid. Drain and chop tomatoes, reserving juice. In another saucepan melt the butter. Add curry powder and cook for 30 seconds. Stir in flour and cook until frothy. Gradually add reserved liquid, wine, reserved tomato juice and chicken stock powder. Bring to the boil, stirring constantly until mixture thickens slightly. Add tomato paste, basil and chopped tomatoes. Bring to the boil. Add mussels, simmer for 10 minutes or until mussels open. Discard any which do not open. Stir in the flaked fish, salt and pepper to taste. Serve garnished with parsley. *Serves 4.* *(Pictured below left.)*

SIR WALTER'S OYSTERS

24 fresh oysters in their shells
1 tablespoon finely chopped
  shallot
2 tablespoons lemon juice
1 teaspoon finely chopped chives

1 teaspoon oil
freshly ground black pepper
2 tablespoons soft butter
2 teaspoons finely chopped parsley
6 slices wholemeal sandwich bread

Arrange oysters in a serving dish. Mix shallot, lemon juice, chives and oil together. Sprinkle over oysters. Grind over black pepper. Mix butter and parsley together. Spread over 2 slices of bread. Top each slice with an unbuttered slice. Remove crusts and cut sandwich into eight triangles. Serve with oysters. *Serves 2 – 4.*

SALMON STEAKS
WITH THAI DIPPING SAUCE

1 teaspoon sesame oil
2 tablespoons lime or lemon juice
4 salmon steaks

THAI DIPPING SAUCE
1 clove garlic
1/4 cup white vinegar
1 tablespoon raw sugar
1/2 teaspoon salt
1/2 teaspoon prepared minced chilli
2 teaspoons finely chopped fresh coriander

Mix sesame oil and lime or lemon juice together. Brush over one side of salmon. Grill for 2 minutes. Turn and brush second side with lime mixture. Grill for 2 minutes or until salmon is just cooked. Serve with Thai Dipping Sauce.

THAI DIPPING SAUCE
Crush, peel and finely chop garlic. Mix garlic, vinegar, sugar, salt, chilli and coriander together. *Serves 4.*

SPANISH PAELLA

6 cups fish or chicken stock
400 g can whole tomatoes in juice
pinch saffron threads
1 single chicken breast
1 pork fillet
2 onions
2 cloves garlic
1 green pepper
3 tablespoons olive oil
3 cups short grain rice
12 mussels in shells
6 whole uncooked prawns
4 lemons

Heat the stock, tomatoes and juice and saffron threads until boiling. Remove skin from chicken breast and discard. Cut chicken into 1 cm strips. Cut pork fillet into 1 cm cubes. Peel onions and chop coarsely. Crush, peel and finely chop garlic. Remove core from green pepper and cut flesh into 1 cm cubes. Heat oil in a paella dish or large frying pan. Sauté chicken and pork until lightly browned. Add onions and peppers and sauté for 2 minutes. Add rice and stir to coat. Cook until rice becomes transparent. Add the hot stock mixture and stir. Simmer for 10 minutes. Add mussels and simmer for 5 minutes or until mussels open. Discard any that do not open. Add prawns and cook for a further 2 minutes. Add more stock if necessary. Remove from heat. Squeeze the juice of two of the lemons over the top of the paella. Cover and stand for 5 minutes. Cut remaining lemons into quarters and use to garnish paella. *Serves 6 – 8.*

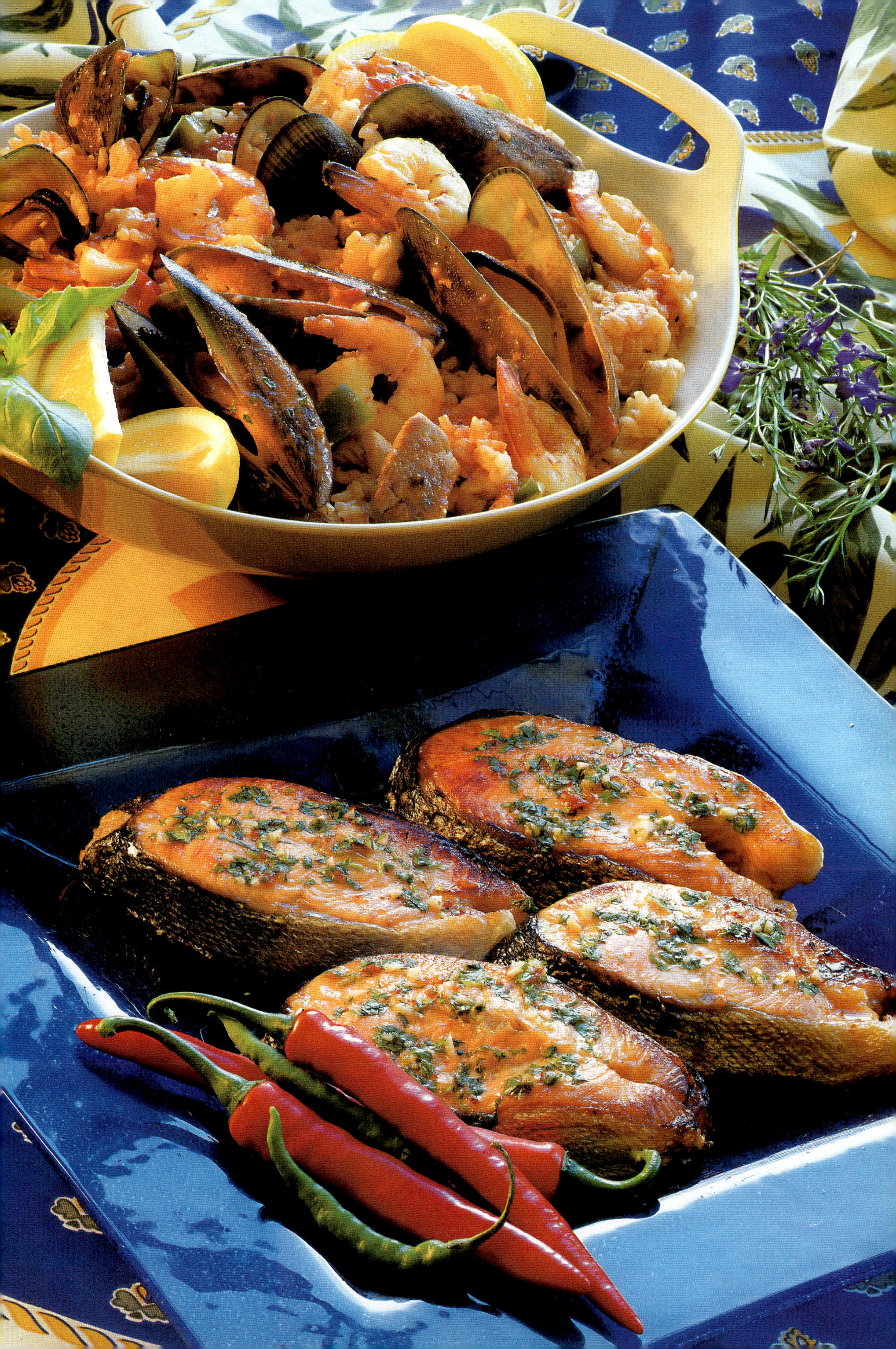

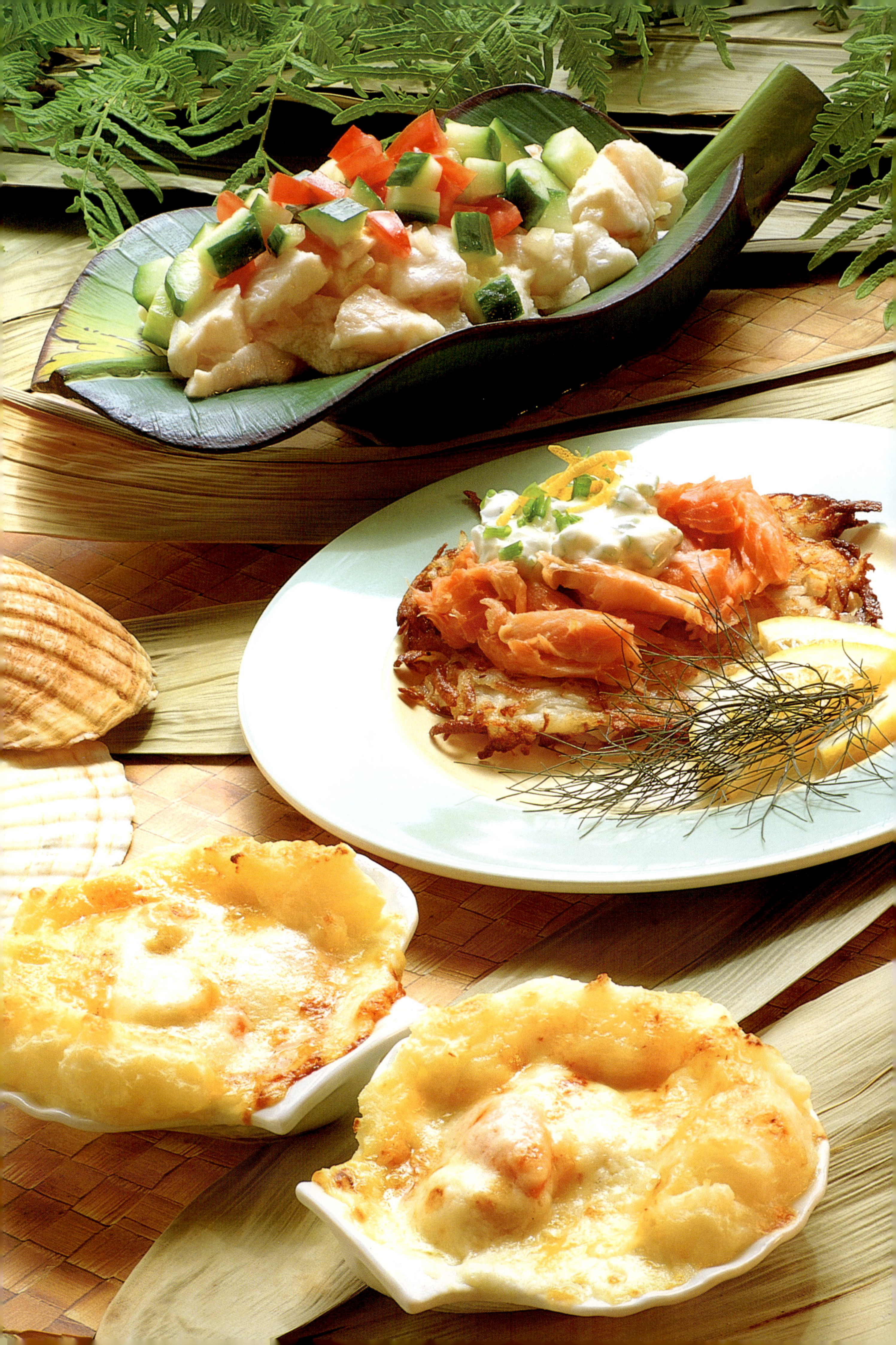

POISSON CRU

500 g skinned and boned firm fish
    fillets – e.g. snapper, John
    Dory, tarakihi, gurnard
1 teaspoon salt
¼ cup lemon juice
1 medium onion, finely chopped
¼ cup coconut milk
2 tomatoes, diced
½ cup chopped cucumber

Cut fish into bite-sized pieces. Sprinkle with salt then lemon juice. Cover and chill for 2 hours or until fish whitens, stirring occasionally. Drain. Stir in onion and coconut milk. Sprinkle tomatoes and cucumber over. Serve chilled. *Serves 4 – 6.*

SCALLOPS MORNAY

2 dozen scallops
2 tablespoons butter
2 tablespoons Champion standard
    plain flour
1½ cups milk
½ cup grated tasty cheese
salt
pepper
2 cups hot mashed potato

Remove any feed tubes from scallops. Set scallops aside. Melt butter in a saucepan. Stir in flour and cook until frothy. Gradually add milk, stirring constantly until mixture boils. Add scallops to sauce. Continue cooking for 5 minutes, stirring occasionally. Remove from heat and stir in half the cheese. Season with salt and pepper to taste. Decorate edge of scallop shells or ovenproof dish with mashed potato. Spoon scallop mixture into serving shells or dish to be used. Sprinkle remaining cheese on top. Grill until golden. *Serves 4 – 6.*
(Main picture, bottom left.)

SMOKED SALMON HASH BROWNS

4 large potatoes
½ teaspoon salt
freshly ground black pepper
2 tablespoons oil
100 g wood-roasted or cold
    smoked salmon
½ cup low-fat sour cream
½ teaspoon grated lemon rind
1 tablespoon chopped fresh chives

Peel potatoes and grate. Place in a sieve and squeeze out as much liquid as possible. Mix in salt and pepper. Heat oil in a large frying pan. Measure ½ cupful of potato and spread into a thin round in the pan. Cook over a medium heat until golden. Turn and cook the other side. Make 3 more hash browns from the remaining mixture. Drain on absorbent paper. Place on a serving dish. Remove skin from wood-roasted salmon or form cold smoked salmon into bunches. Arrange a quarter of the salmon on each hash brown. Mix sour cream, lemon rind and chives together. Serve with salmon and hash browns. *Serves 4.*

SQUID RINGS

500 g squid rings
2 cloves garlic, crushed
2 eggs
1 tablespoon Edmonds Fielder's
　cornflour
1 tablespoon milk
2 cups toasted breadcrumbs,
　approximately
oil for deep-frying

Put squid and garlic in a bowl. Leave for 15 minutes. Beat eggs, cornflour and milk together. Dip squid rings into egg mixture. Coat with breadcrumbs. Deep-fry in hot oil for 2 minutes or until golden. Do not overcook as this will toughen the squid. Serve with a dipping sauce. **Serves 4.**

THAI FISH CAKES

185 g can tuna in brine
1 teaspoon ground coriander
1 teaspoon Thai fish sauce
1/4 cup coconut cream
1 egg

2 tablespoons chopped fresh coriander
1 teaspoon prepared minced chilli
1 1/2 cups soft breadcrumbs
1/2 teaspoon salt
1/4 cup peanut oil

Drain tuna. Place tuna, coriander, fish sauce, coconut cream, egg, fresh coriander, chilli, breadcrumbs and salt in a food processor. Process until combined but not paste-like. Measure tablespoonsful of mixture and cook in hot oil in a frying pan until golden on both sides. Drain on absorbent paper and serve hot. *Makes 26.*

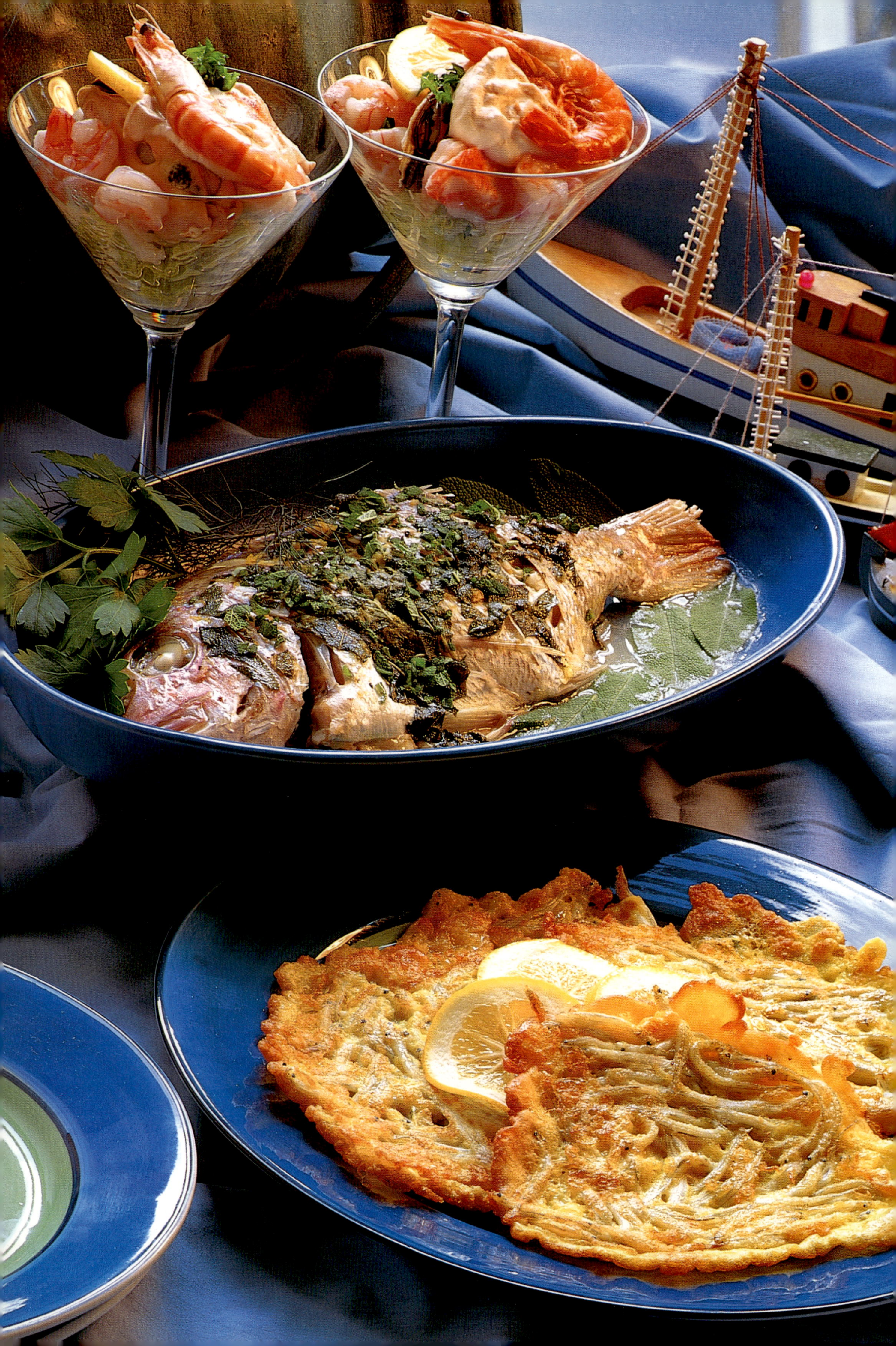

SEAFOOD COCKTAIL

2 cups mixed seafood – shrimps,
   crab, prawns, oysters, crayfish
1 cup cream
1/4 cup tomato sauce
2 teaspoons lemon juice
white pepper
1 cup shredded lettuce
paprika or chopped parsley

Combine seafood. Chill while preparing sauce. Put cream in a bowl and beat until thickened slightly, about the consistency of raw egg white. Beat in tomato sauce, lemon juice and pepper. Place a small amount of lettuce into individual serving dishes. Divide seafood mixture evenly among the prepared dishes. Spoon cream mixture over seafood. Garnish with paprika. Replace cream with natural unsweetened yoghurt and 1/2 teaspoon sugar if wished. **Serves 4 – 5.** *(Main picture, top right.)*

BAKED LEMON AND SAGE FISH

1 whole fish, about 1 kg
1 teaspoon grated lemon rind
1/4 cup lemon juice
2 tablespoons melted butter
2 tablespoons chopped fresh sage
1/2 teaspoon salt
freshly ground black pepper

Remove scales from fish using the back of a knife to run along the skin of the fish. Wash and dry fish. Cut 4 slashes in the top and bottom of the fish. Mix lemon rind, juice, melted butter, sage, salt and pepper together. Brush over skin, into slashes and inside body cavity of fish. Wrap in a layer of baking paper then a layer of foil. Bake at 190°C for 20 to 25 minutes or until fish flakes easily. **Serves 4.** *(Main picture, middle right.)*

WHITEBAIT FRITTERS

2 tablespoons Edmonds Fielder's
   cornflour
1/2 teaspoon Edmonds baking
   powder
1/2 teaspoon salt
2 eggs
1 tablespoon milk, approximately
125 g whitebait or strips of
   firm fish – e.g. lemon fish,
   trevally, orange roughy
oil for shallow frying
lemon wedges

Sift cornflour, baking powder and salt into bowl. Add eggs and milk to mix to a smooth batter. Drain whitebait well. Stir in whitebait or fish. Coat well with egg mixture. Heat oil in a large frying pan. Add fritters and cook until golden on both sides. Drain on absorbent paper. Serve with lemon. **Makes 4 fritters.**

MEAT

BEEF OLIVES

1 cup soft breadcrumbs
1/4 cup chopped prunes
1 small onion, finely chopped
1/2 teaspoon grated lemon rind
1/2 teaspoon dried thyme
6 pieces beef schnitzel

2 tablespoons oil
2 tablespoons Champion standard
    plain flour
3/4 cup beef stock
2 tablespoons soy sauce

Combine breadcrumbs, prunes, onion, lemon rind and thyme. Lay pieces of schnitzel out flat. Divide breadcrumb mixture evenly among pieces of meat. Spread each piece of meat with breadcrumb mixture then roll up like a sponge roll. Secure with toothpicks. Heat oil in a frying pan. Add beef olives and brown on all sides. Transfer to a casserole dish. Stir flour into frying pan and cook for 1 minute. Gradually add stock, stirring constantly. Bring to the boil. Add soy sauce. Pour this over beef olives. Cook at 160°C for 30 to 40 minutes or until meat is tender. Remove toothpicks before serving. **Serves 4.**

PORK OLIVES
Use pork schnitzel in place of beef. It may be necessary to double the pieces of schnitzel as pork is usually smaller in size.

BEEF STROGANOFF

500 g rump steak
2 tablespoons butter
1 tablespoon oil
1 onion, sliced
150 g mushrooms, sliced

1/4 cup white wine
3/4 cup sour cream
1 tablespoon lemon juice
salt
pepper

Trim fat from meat. Cut meat into thin strips against the grain. Heat butter and oil in a frying pan. Add meat and quickly brown on both sides. Remove from pan and set aside. Add onion and mushrooms to pan. Cook until onion is clear. Return meat to pan. Add wine and sour cream. Reheat gently. Add lemon juice. Season with salt and pepper to taste. Serve with rice. **Serves 4.**

BEEF OR LAMB SATAYS WITH PEANUT SAUCE

500 g rump steak or lamb steaks
satay sticks
2 tablespoons chilli oil

PEANUT SAUCE
1 small onion
1 teaspoon peanut oil

1 teaspoon prepared minced chilli
1 teaspoon ground cumin
2 teaspoons ground coriander
3/4 cup crunchy peanut butter
1/4 cup lemon juice
2 tablespoons soy sauce

Trim fat from meat. Cut meat into 0.5 cm strips. Thread meat strips onto satay sticks. Brush with chilli oil. Grill or barbecue until preferred doneness. Set aside. For sauce, peel onion and chop finely. Heat oil in a small saucepan and sauté onion for 5 minutes or until clear. Add chilli, cumin and coriander and cook for about 1 minute or until spices smell fragrant. Remove from heat and stir in peanut butter, lemon juice and soy sauce. Mix until combined. Serve warm or cold with satays. **Serves 4.** *(Pictured below left.)*

BOEUF BOURGUIGNON

750 g chuck steak
2 tablespoons Champion standard
    plain flour
salt
pepper
2 tablespoons oil
8 pickling onions
2 rashers bacon

2 cloves garlic, crushed
3/4 cup red wine
1/2 cup beef stock
4 carrots, quartered lengthwise
sprig parsley
sprig thyme
bay leaf

Trim fat from meat. Cut meat into serving-sized pieces. Combine flour, salt and pepper. Coat meat in seasoned flour. Heat oil in a flameproof casserole dish. Add onions and bacon and cook until golden. Using a slotted spoon, remove from pan and set aside. Add half the meat and quickly brown on all sides. Repeat with remaining meat. Return onions and bacon to pan with garlic. Add wine and stock, stirring well. Add carrots. Make a bouquet garni from parsley, thyme and bay leaf. Add to casserole. Cover and cook at 180°C for 1 1/2 to 2 hours or until meat is tender. Serve with French bread and salad. **Serves 4.**

CHILLI AND CORIANDER MARINATED STEAK

4 pieces eye fillet, scotch fillet
  or rump steak
¼ cup sweet chilli sauce
2 tablespoons soy sauce
2 tablespoons chopped
  fresh coriander

Trim fat from steak if necessary. Mix chilli sauce, soy sauce and coriander together in a shallow dish. Place steak in marinade and turn to coat. Leave for 2 hours at room temperature or refrigerate overnight. Grill or barbecue to preferred doneness. *Serves 4.*
(Pictured below left.)

CORNED BEEF

1 kg corned silverside
1 bay leaf
sprig parsley
4 black peppercorns
1 tablespoon golden syrup
1 thinly peeled strip orange rind
1 tablespoon DYC malt vinegar

Put silverside in a saucepan. Add bay leaf, parsley, peppercorns, golden syrup, orange rind and vinegar. Barely cover with water. Cover and bring to the boil then simmer gently for 1 to 1½ hours or until meat is tender. Drain. Some of the cooking liquid can be used in a sauce to serve with the meat. If wished, serve hot or cold with white sauce, mustard sauce or plum sauce. *Serves 6.*

GINGER BEEF STIR-FRY

500 g skirt steak
1 tablespoon oil
1 tablespoon soy sauce
2 teaspoons grated root ginger
2 tablespoons oil
1 red pepper, cubed
1 green pepper, cubed

4 spring onions, sliced
2 teaspoons soy sauce
2 tablespoons DYC white vinegar
2 teaspoons Edmonds
   Fielder's cornflour
½ teaspoon sugar
¼ cup beef stock

Trim fat from meat. Cut into thin strips against the grain. Put meat, first measure of oil, first measure of soy sauce and ginger in a bowl. Leave to marinate for 30 minutes. Heat half the second measure of oil in a wok. Add meat and quickly stir-fry until browned. Remove from wok. Repeat with remaining oil and meat. Return meat to wok. Add peppers and spring onions. Stir-fry until vegetables are bright in colour. In a bowl mix second measure of soy sauce, vinegar, cornflour, sugar and stock to a smooth paste. Add to wok and cook for 1 minute or until liquid boils and thickens. *Serves 6.*

INDIAN BEEF CURRY

500 g beef topside
1 onion
2 cloves garlic
2 tablespoons peanut oil
2 tablespoons finely chopped fresh
   ginger
2 teaspoons ground cumin

2 teaspoons garam masala
2 teaspoons ground coriander
½ teaspoon ground cloves
2 cups beef stock
1 cup natural unsweetened
   yoghurt
8 poppadoms

Trim fat from meat and cut meat into 2 cm cubes. Peel onion and chop finely. Crush, peel and chop garlic. Heat oil in a large saucepan and sauté onion and garlic for 5 minutes or until clear. Add ginger, cumin, garam masala, coriander and cloves. Sauté for 1 minute or until spices smell fragrant. Add meat and stock. Cover and simmer for 1 to 1½ hours or until meat is tender and stock reduced to about ½ cup. Stir in yoghurt. Bring to the boil and then reduce heat. Cook poppadoms, two at a time, in the microwave on high power for 1 minute or until poppadoms are crisp and have changed from a raw to a cooked look all over. Alternatively, cook poppadoms to packet directions in hot oil. Serve curry with cooked poppadoms and steamed rice. *Serves 4.*

LAMB RACKS WITH REDCURRANT SAUCE

4 lamb racks (4 chops each)
1 cup soft breadcrumbs
¼ cup chopped fresh herbs such as chives, parsley and dill
1 egg
1 tablespoon lemon juice
1 teaspoon grated lemon rind

REDCURRANT SAUCE
1 small onion
1 teaspoon oil
1 cup redcurrant jelly
2 tablespoons red wine vinegar
freshly ground black pepper
1 tablespoon drained washed capers

Trim lamb racks, removing excess fat if necessary. Mix breadcrumbs, herbs, egg, lemon juice and lemon rind together until well combined. Press onto the fat side of the lamb racks. Place in a roasting dish, breadcrumb side up. Bake at 180°C for 25 to 30 minutes or until meat is cooked to preferred doneness and crumbs are golden. Serve with Redcurrant Sauce. *Serves 4 – 6.*

REDCURRANT SAUCE
Peel onion and chop finely. Heat oil in a small saucepan and sauté onion for 5 minutes or until clear. Remove from heat and mix in redcurrant jelly, vinegar, pepper and capers.

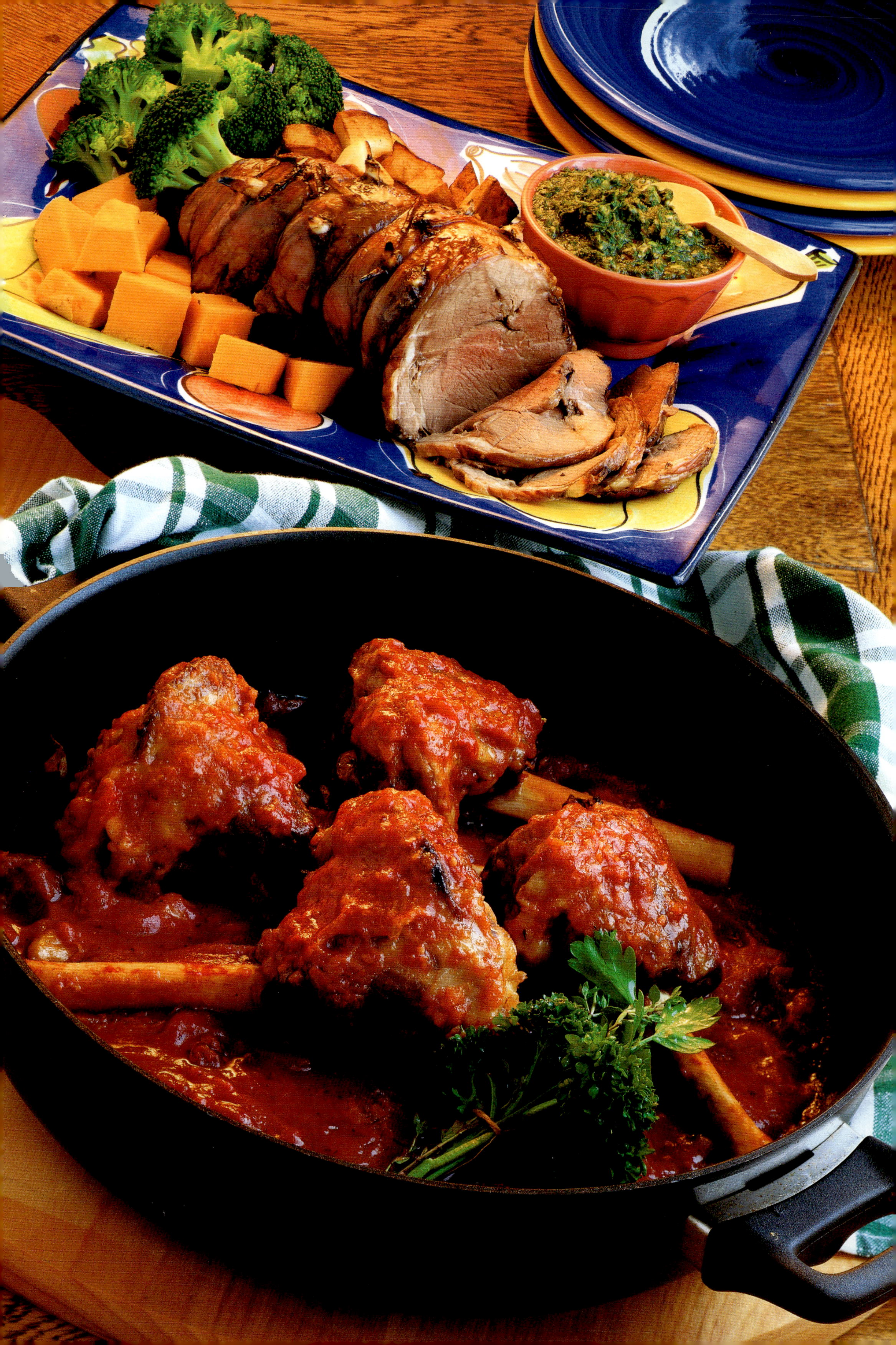

LAMB SHANKS IN RED WINE

4 lamb shanks or knuckles
8 cloves garlic
425 g can tomatoes in juice
2 tablespoons tomato paste
1 cup red wine
2 bouquet garni

4 potatoes
2 x 300 g can chickpeas
2 tablespoons tahini
salt
freshly ground black pepper
2 tablespoons chopped parsley

Place lamb shanks and washed unpeeled garlic in a roasting dish. Bake at 200°C for 15 minutes to draw out the fat. Drain on absorbent paper. Place shanks and garlic in a large casserole or ovenproof dish. Roughly chop tomatoes. Mix in tomato paste and add to shanks with wine and bouquet garni. Cover and bake at 180°C for 2 hours. Peel potatoes and cook in boiling, salted water until tender. Drain, reserving a little cooking water to make a smooth creamy mixture. Drain chickpeas and purée with tahini. Mix mashed potato and chickpea purée together until well combined. Season lamb and potato mixture with salt and pepper. Serve lamb and sauce on a bed of potato and chickpea purée. Garnish with chopped parsley. *Serves 4.* *(Pictured below left.)*

ROAST LAMB WITH FRESH MINT CHUTNEY

1 kg shank end leg of lamb
3 cloves garlic
8 strips lemon rind

FRESH MINT CHUTNEY
2 spring onions
1 clove garlic

1 cup firmly packed mint leaves
1/2 teaspoon salt
1 teaspoon sugar
1 teaspoon garam masala
1/4 cup lemon juice
1 teaspoon prepared minced chilli

Remove skin from lamb, leaving a thin layer of fat. Crush garlic, peel and cut into slivers. Cut slashes in lamb fat and push a garlic sliver in each. Arrange lemon rind over. Bake at 180°C for 1 1/2 hours for medium-rare lamb or until preferred doneness. Serve sliced, accompanied by Fresh Mint Chutney. *Serves 4 – 6.*

FRESH MINT CHUTNEY

Trim spring onions and chop roughly. Crush and peel garlic. Place spring onions, garlic, mint, salt, sugar, garam masala, lemon juice and prepared minced chilli into a food processor or blender. Process until smooth.

SHEPHERD'S PIE

1 tablespoon oil
1 onion, chopped
500 g mince
2 tablespoons Champion standard plain flour
1 tablespoon tomato sauce
1 tablespoon chutney or relish
¾ cup beef stock

3 potatoes, peeled and chopped
1 tablespoon butter
1 tablespoon finely chopped onion
½ cup grated tasty cheese
salt
black pepper

Heat oil in a large frying pan. Add onion and cook until clear. Add mince and cook until well browned, stirring constantly. Pour off excess fat. Stir in flour and cook for 1 minute. Add tomato sauce, chutney and stock. Bring to the boil, reduce heat and simmer for 5 minutes. Set aside. Cook potatoes in boiling, salted water until tender. Drain and heat for a few minutes to dry off excess moisture. Shake the pan frequently during this time. Mash potato. Add butter, onion and half the cheese, mixing until smooth and creamy. Season with salt and pepper to taste. Put mince into a pie dish. Top with potato mixture. Sprinkle with remaining cheese. Bake at 180°C for 20 minutes or until golden and heated through. **Serves 4.** *(Pictured below left.)*

SWEET AND SOUR PORK

500 g pork pieces
2 cloves garlic, crushed
2 tablespoons oil
2 small onions, quartered
½ cup chicken stock
225 g can pineapple pieces in syrup
1 tablespoon Edmonds Fielder's cornflour

¼ cup tomato sauce
½ teaspoon grated root ginger
2 tablespoons DYC white vinegar
2 tablespoons brown sugar
½ cup chopped red pepper
½ cup chopped cucumber
½ cup baby sweetcorn
100 g mushrooms, quartered

Trim fat from pork and cut into 2 cm pieces. Peel garlic and chop finely. Heat oil in a saucepan or wok. Add onion and garlic and cook until onion is clear. Remove from pan. Add half the pork pieces and quickly brown on all sides. Remove from pan. Repeat with remaining meat. Return meat and onions to pan. Add stock and bring to the boil. Cover and cook gently for 30 minutes or until meat is tender. Drain pineapple, reserving juice. Combine juice and cornflour, mixing until smooth. Add pineapple pieces, tomato sauce, ginger, vinegar, sugar, pepper, cucumber, sweetcorn and mushrooms to pan. Cook for 5 minutes. Return to the boil. Stir in cornflour mixture and boil for 2 minutes or until mixture thickens slightly. Serve with rice or noodles. **Serves 4 – 6.**

VEAL CORDON BLEU

8 small pieces wiener schnitzel
2 large slices ham
4 slices mozzarella cheese
½ cup Champion standard
   plain flour
salt
pepper
2 eggs
¼ cup water
1½ cups toasted breadcrumbs
50 g butter
2 tablespoons oil

Put a piece of plastic wrap over one schnitzel at a time. Using a rolling pin, roll the meat thinner. Repeat with remaining meat. Cut ham in half. On half the pieces of meat, place a piece of ham, top with a slice of cheese. Place another piece of meat on top, pressing edges together. Combine flour, salt and pepper to taste. Coat schnitzels in seasoned flour. Beat eggs and water together. Dip schnitzels in this. Coat in breadcrumbs. Repeat with egg and breadcrumbs. Heat butter and oil together in a large frying pan. Add schnitzel and cook for 5 minutes each side or until golden. **Serves 4.**

CHICKEN CORDON BLEU

Use single boneless chicken breasts instead of veal schnitzel. Roll thinly then proceed as above.

CHICKEN

CHICKEN AND APRICOT FILO PARCELS

1 small onion
1 teaspoon oil
1 tablespoon grated root ginger
1 cup chopped dried apricots
¼ cup orange juice
4 single chicken breasts
8 sheets filo pastry
1½ cups soft breadcrumbs
¼ cup melted butter
1 tablespoon sesame seeds

Peel onion and chop finely. Heat oil in a saucepan and sauté onion and ginger for 5 minutes or until onion is clear. Add apricots and orange juice. Simmer for 5 minutes or until pulpy. Cool. Remove skin from chicken and cut a long pocket in the side of each breast. Fill with apricot mixture. Cut filo pastry sheets crossways. Keep pastry under a damp tea-towel until ready to work with it. Sprinkle breadcrumbs between 4 squares of pastry. Place chicken breast on top of the pastry layer. Fold pastry over chicken to make a neat parcel. Place seam side down on a greased oven tray. Brush with melted butter and sprinkle with sesame seeds. Bake at 190°C for 20 minutes or until golden and cooked. **Serves 4.** *(Main picture, bottom left.)*

CHICKEN AND AVOCADO SALAD

2 avocados, peeled and sliced
2 tablespoons lemon juice
2 cups diced cooked chicken
   or smoked chicken
¼ cup sliced celery
¼ cup raisins
2 oranges, peeled and sliced
¼ cup mayonnaise
lettuce leaves

Toss avocados in lemon juice. Combine avocado, chicken, celery, raisins, oranges and mayonnaise. Toss to combine. Place on a bed of lettuce leaves. Chill before serving. **Serves 4.**

CHICKEN AND PESTO BAKE

8 chicken drumsticks
¼ cup basil or sundried tomato
   pesto
¾ cup toasted breadcrumbs
fresh basil

Remove skin from chicken. Brush or spread drumsticks with pesto. Coat with breadcrumbs. Place in a greased roasting dish and bake at 190°C for 35 minutes or until juices run clear when tested. Serve scattered with torn fresh basil leaves. **Serves 4.**

CHICKEN PAPRIKA

4 chicken breasts
2 tablespoons oil
1 large onion, chopped
2 teaspoons paprika
1 tablespoon Champion standard plain flour
1 cup chicken stock
250 g pot sour cream or 300 ml cream
1 tablespoon lemon juice
salt
black pepper

Remove skin and fat from chicken. Heat oil in a large frying pan. Add chicken and quickly brown on all sides. Remove from pan and set aside. Add onion and cook until clear. Stir in paprika and cook for 30 seconds. Stir in flour and cook, stirring, for 1 minute. Gradually add stock, stirring constantly. Bring to the boil. Return chicken to pan. Cover, reduce heat and simmer gently for 15 minutes. Stir in sour cream. Continue cooking gently for a further 10 minutes or until juices run clear when tested. Add lemon juice. Season with salt and pepper to taste. Serve with rice. **Serves 4.** *(Pictured below left.)*

CHICKEN PIE

500 g boneless skinless chicken meat
1 onion
2 cloves garlic
25 g butter
1 carrot
1 cup frozen peas
3 tablespoons Champion standard plain flour
2 cups low-fat milk
2 tablespoons chopped parsley
salt
freshly ground black pepper
400 g packet flaky pastry

Cut the chicken into bite-sized pieces. Peel onion and chop finely. Crush, peel and chop garlic. Melt butter in a medium saucepan and sauté onion and garlic for 5 minutes or until onion is clear. Peel carrot and grate. Add carrot and chicken to saucepan. Stir-fry for 5 minutes. Add peas. Mix flour to a paste with a little of the measured milk. Add milk to saucepan. Bring to the boil. Stir in the flour paste. Cook stirring until mixture boils and thickens. Stir in parsley, salt and pepper. Leave to cool. Cut one-third from the pastry. Roll larger piece of pastry out on a lightly floured board to fit a 24 cm pie plate. Trim edges to neaten. Spoon in cold chicken filling. Roll out remaining pastry to make a lid. Wet edges and press bottom and top edges together. Decorate top with trimmings if wished. Make two holes in centre of pastry top. Bake at 200°C for 30 to 40 minutes or until pastry is cooked and golden. Serve hot or cold. **Serves 4.**

CHICKEN STIR-FRY WITH CASHEWS

2 single boneless chicken breasts
1 tablespoon Edmonds Fielder's
    cornflour
1 egg white
2 tablespoons oil
2 stalks celery, sliced
6 spring onions, sliced
100 g button mushrooms,
    quartered
2 teaspoons grated root ginger
1/2 cup chicken stock
1/2 teaspoon sugar
2 teaspoons Edmonds Fielder's
    cornflour
1 tablespoon dry sherry
1/4 cup roasted cashew nuts

Remove skin and fat from chicken. Cut meat in 2.5 cm cubes. Coat in first measure of cornflour then in lightly beaten egg white. Heat oil in a wok or large frying pan. Add chicken and cook until crisp and golden. Remove chicken from pan with a slotted spoon. Set aside. Add celery to pan and stir-fry until just tender. Add spring onions, mushrooms and ginger. Stir-fry until spring onions are bright green in colour. Blend stock, sugar, second measure of cornflour and sherry together. Add to pan. Cook, stirring until mixture boils and thickens slightly. Add chicken and cashews. Stir to heat through. **Serves 4.**

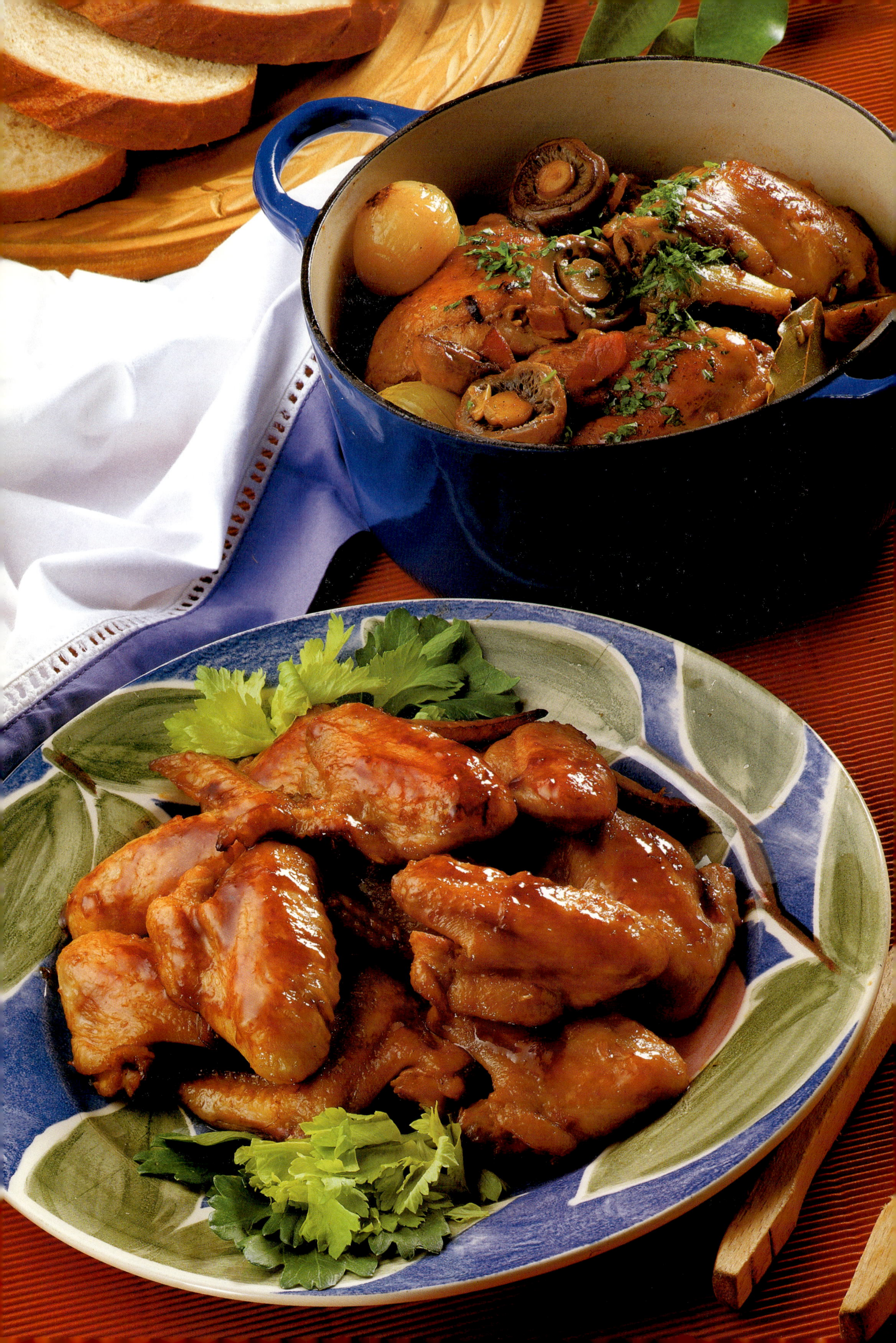

COQ-AU-VIN

25 g butter
2 rashers bacon, chopped
8 pieces chicken
12 pickling onions
100 g button mushrooms
2 tablespoons brandy
1½ cups red wine
2 cloves garlic, crushed
1 tablespoon tomato paste

1 bay leaf
sprig thyme
sprig parsley
salt
pepper
2 tablespoons Champion standard plain flour
25 g butter

Melt first measure of butter in a flameproof casserole dish or saucepan. Add bacon and cook for 4 minutes. Remove from pan. Remove skin from chicken. Add to pan and cook until browned on both sides. Remove from pan. Peel onions, add to pan and cook until golden. Return bacon and chicken to pan. Add mushrooms. Pour brandy over chicken. Stir in wine, garlic and tomato paste. Make a bouquet garni with bay leaf, thyme and parsley. Add to saucepan. Bring to the boil. Cover, reduce heat and simmer gently for 45 minutes or until chicken is tender. Season with salt and pepper to taste. Put flour and second measure of butter into a small bowl. Mix together to form a paste called *beurre manié*. Remove chicken from pan and keep warm. Bring cooking liquid to the boil and whisk in the *beurre manié* a little at a time, cooking gently until sauce is smooth and thickened slightly. Remove bouquet garni. Return chicken to the pan and serve. **Serves 4.**

MARINATED CHICKEN WINGS

3 cloves garlic, crushed
3 tablespoons soy sauce
2 tablespoons liquid honey
1 tablespoon tomato sauce
2 teaspoons grated root ginger
500 g chicken wings

Combine garlic, soy sauce, honey, tomato sauce and ginger. Brush chicken wings well with this. Leave to marinate for 1 hour. Grill for 8 to 10 minutes or until golden, turning once during cooking time. Alternatively place wings in roasting dish. Cook at 200°C for 10 minutes or until crisp and golden. Serve hot or cold. **Serves 4.**

ROAST STUFFED CHICKEN

1 no. 8 chicken

Remove giblets from chicken. Use to make stock. Spoon the stuffing into the cavity of the bird and secure opening with skewers. Bake 180°C for 1 hour or until juices run clear.

BASIC BREAD STUFFING

3 cups soft breadcrumbs
1 onion, finely chopped
1 teaspoon dried sage
2 tablespoons melted butter
1 egg
salt
pepper

Combine breadcrumbs, onion, sage, butter and egg in bowl. Season with salt and pepper to taste. *Makes about 1 cup.*

SAUSAGE-MEAT STUFFING
Add 200 g sausage meat to half a quantity of basic stuffing.

ORANGE AND ROSEMARY STUFFING
Add 2 tablespoons grated orange rind and 2 teaspoons rosemary.

APRICOT STUFFING
Add $1/2$ cup chopped dried apricots which have been soaked in $1/4$ cup orange juice for 2 hours.

THAI CHICKEN CURRY

500 g boneless skinless chicken meat
1 onion
2 cloves garlic
1 tablespoon peanut oil
1 tablespoon prepared green curry paste
425 g can light coconut cream
$1/4$ cup chicken stock
2 tablespoons chopped fresh coriander or parsley
steamed rice for 4
$1/2$ cup roasted peanuts

Cut chicken into pieces if necessary. Peel onion and chop finely. Crush, peel and chop garlic. Heat oil in a large saucepan. Sauté onion and garlic for 5 minutes or until clear. Add curry paste and sauté for 1 minute or until spices smell fragrant. Add chicken, coconut cream and stock. Cook for 20 minutes or until chicken is just cooked. Stir in coriander or parsley. Serve with steamed rice garnished with roasted peanuts. *Serves 4.*

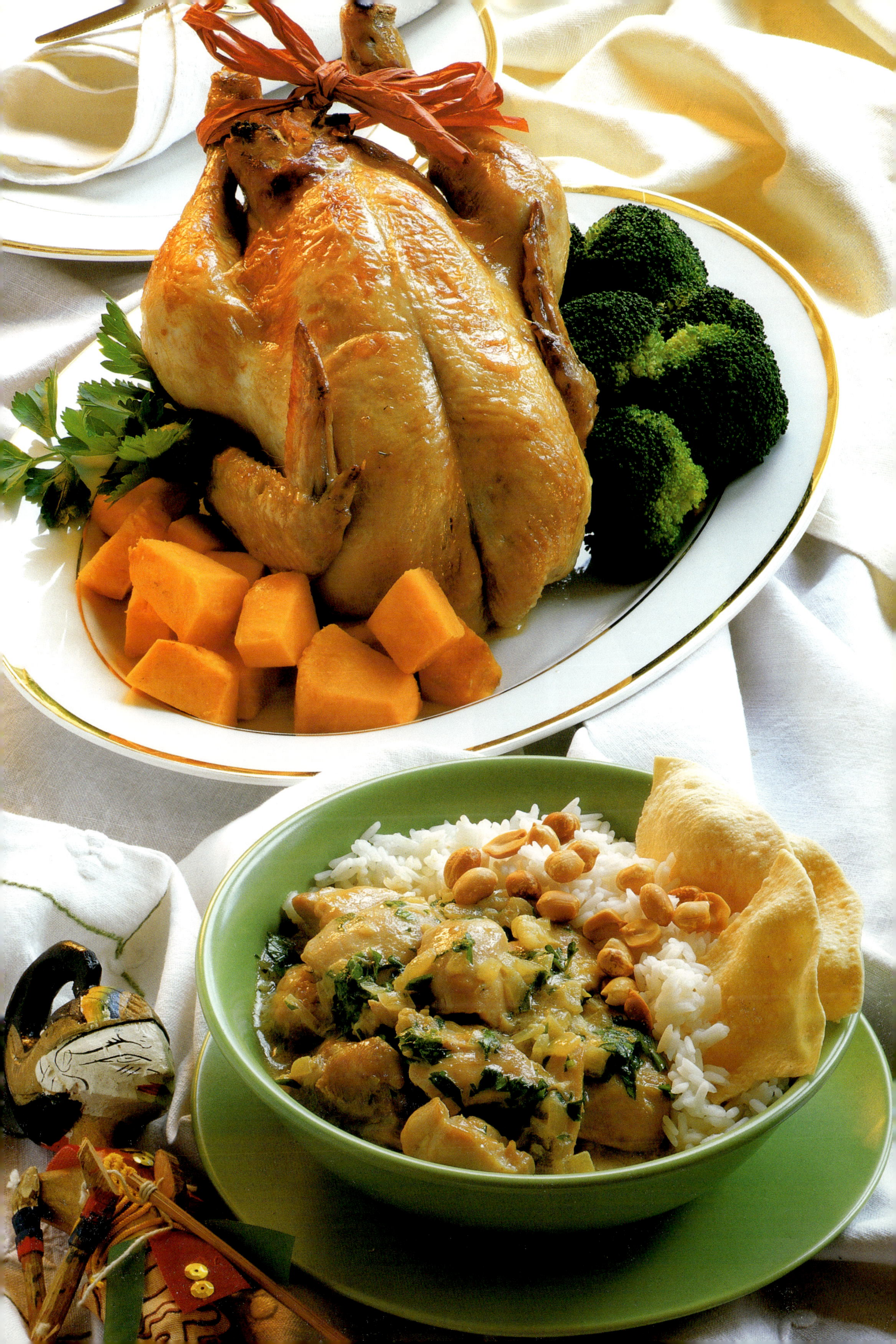

VEGETABLES

CAESAR SALAD

4 cloves garlic
1/4 cup olive oil
3 cups stale French bread,
  cut into cubes
4 eggs
1 medium cos lettuce
1/4 cup lemon juice

1/2 teaspoon salt
1/4 cup olive oil
1/2 teaspoon Worcestershire sauce
1/2 cup grated or shaved
  parmesan cheese
8 anchovy fillets

Crush, peel and mash garlic. Mix 3 cloves of garlic with first measure of oil so the garlic infuses the oil. Place oil in a roasting dish. Place in a 190°C oven for 5 minutes. Add bread cubes and toss to coat bread. Bake at 190°C for 10 to 15 minutes or until golden, turning occasionally. Soft boil eggs in boiling water for 4 minutes. Drain and run under cold water. Wash lettuce and dry. Tear leaves into pieces and place in bowls or on a platter. Mix remaining garlic clove with lemon juice, salt, oil and Worcestershire sauce. When ready to serve, pour this dressing over lettuce. Shell eggs and chop roughly. Add to salad with bread, parmesan cheese and anchovy fillets. *Serves 4 – 6.* (Pictured below left.)

GREEK SALAD

1 lettuce
1 green pepper, sliced
1 small onion, sliced
3 tomatoes, quartered
1/2 cup sliced celery
1/2 diced cucumber
1/2 cup pitted black olives
100 g fetta cheese, cubed

DRESSING
1/4 cup olive oil
1 clove garlic, crushed
2 tablespoons DYC spiced vinegar
1/4 teaspoon sugar

Tear lettuce into bite-sized pieces and place in a salad bowl. Add pepper, onion, tomatoes, celery and cucumber. Pour dressing over and toss to coat. Decorate with olives and fetta cheese. *Serves 4 – 6.*

DRESSING
Put all ingredients in a screw-top jar. Shake vigorously to combine just before using.

GRILLED VEGETABLES WITH VINAIGRETTE

8 brown mushroom flats
1 red pepper
1 green pepper
4 courgettes
12 asparagus spears
oil

VINAIGRETTE
1 clove garlic
3/4 cup olive oil
1/4 cup DYC white vinegar
1 teaspoon wholegrain mustard
1/4 teaspoon salt
2 tablespoons chopped fresh herbs
such as chives, parsley or basil

Wipe mushrooms. Cut peppers in half and remove core and seeds. Cut into quarters. Trim courgettes. Cut in half lengthwise. Snap woody ends from asparagus. Brush vegetables with oil and grill under a hot grill or over the barbecue until golden. Place on a serving platter and pour over vinaigrette. Serve warm or cold. **Serves 4.** *(Pictured below left.)*

VINAIGRETTE
Crush and peel garlic. Shake oil, vinegar, mustard, salt, herbs and garlic together in a screw-top jar until combined.

RATATOUILLE

1/4 cup olive oil
6 medium tomatoes, blanched and chopped
1/2 teaspoon salt
black pepper
1/4 teaspoon sugar

1 large onion, sliced
2 cloves garlic, crushed
1 green pepper, sliced
250 g courgettes, sliced
1 eggplant, chopped

Heat half the oil in a small saucepan. Add tomatoes, salt, pepper to taste and sugar. Cook for 10 minutes or until sauce consistency, stirring frequently. Heat remaining oil in a large frying pan or saucepan. Add onion and garlic and cook until onion is clear. Stir in green pepper, courgettes and eggplant. Cover and cook slowly until vegetables are tender, stirring frequently. Add tomato mixture to the vegetables. Stir to combine. Serve hot. **Serves 6.**

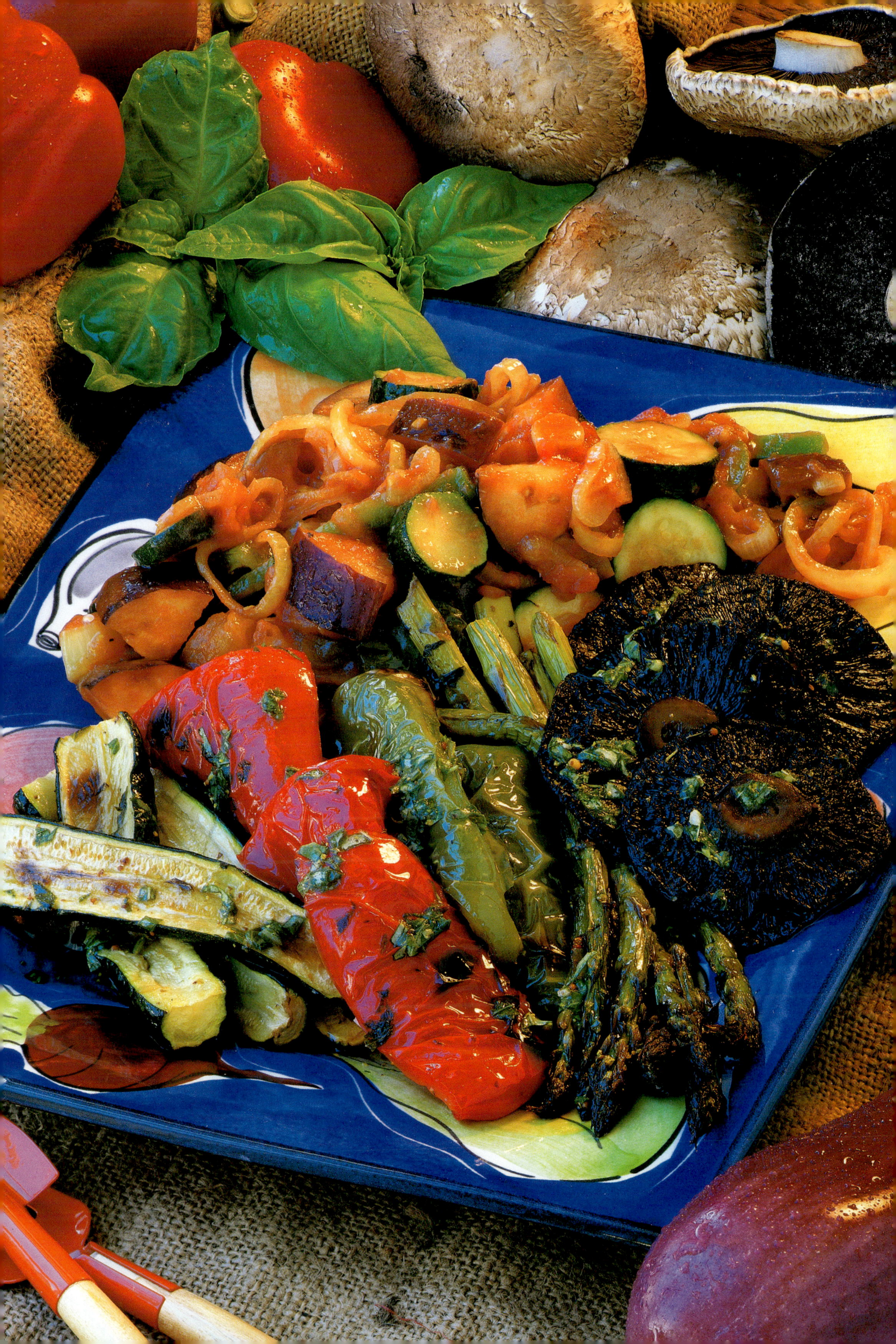

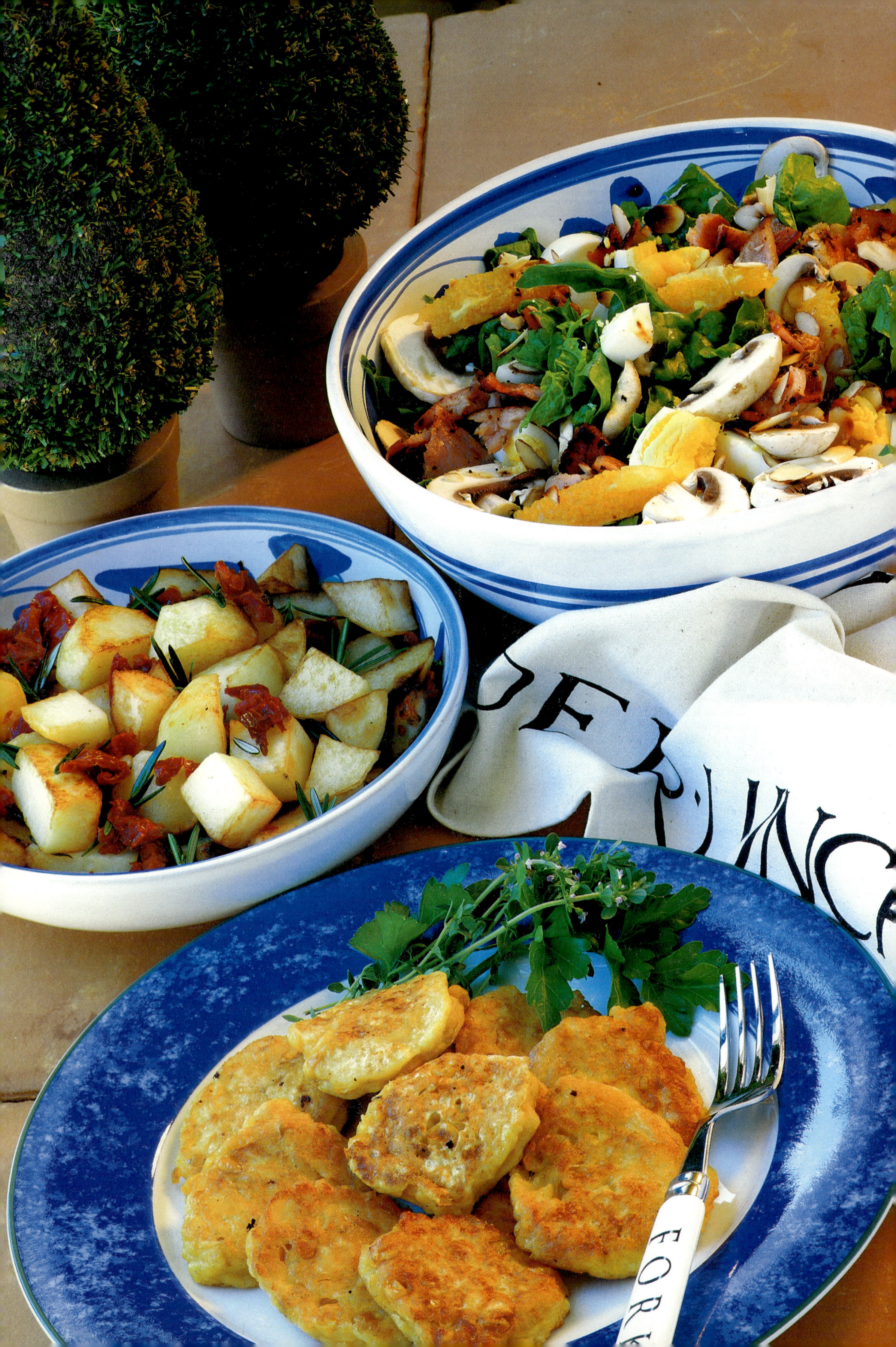

SWEETCORN FRITTERS

3/4 cup Champion standard
    plain flour
1 teaspoon Edmonds
    baking powder
1/2 teaspoon salt
black pepper
1 egg
440 g can cream-style sweetcorn
2 tablespoons oil

Sift flour, baking powder, salt and pepper to taste into a bowl. Add egg, mixing to combine. Stir in sweetcorn. Heat oil in a frying pan. Drop tablespoons of corn mixture into pan. Cook until golden then turn and cook the other side. Drain on absorbent paper. Serve hot. *Makes 20.*

SPINACH SALAD

1 bunch spinach
6 to 8 mushrooms, sliced
2 spring onions, sliced
1 orange, peeled and segmented
3 rashers bacon, cooked and diced
1/4 cup French dressing
2 hard-boiled eggs, chopped
1/4 cup toasted flaked almonds

Tear spinach into bite-sized pieces and place in a salad bowl. Add mushrooms, spring onions, orange segments and bacon. Chill before serving. Add French dressing and toss. Garnish with eggs and flaked almonds. *Serves 4 – 6.*

TUSCAN POTATOES WITH SUNDRIED TOMATOES

6 medium potatoes
2 cloves garlic
3 tablespoons oil drained from
    sundried tomatoes, or olive oil
1 tablespoon fresh rosemary leaves
    or 1 1/2 teaspoons dried
    rosemary
1/4 cup drained, chopped sundried
    tomatoes

Peel potatoes and cut into cubes. Crush, peel and finely chop garlic. Heat oil in a roasting dish or electric frying pan. Add potatoes and cook at 180°C for 20 minutes, turning frequently, until lightly golden on all sides and cooked. Add garlic, rosemary and tomatoes. Cook for a further 5 minutes. *Serves 4 – 6.*

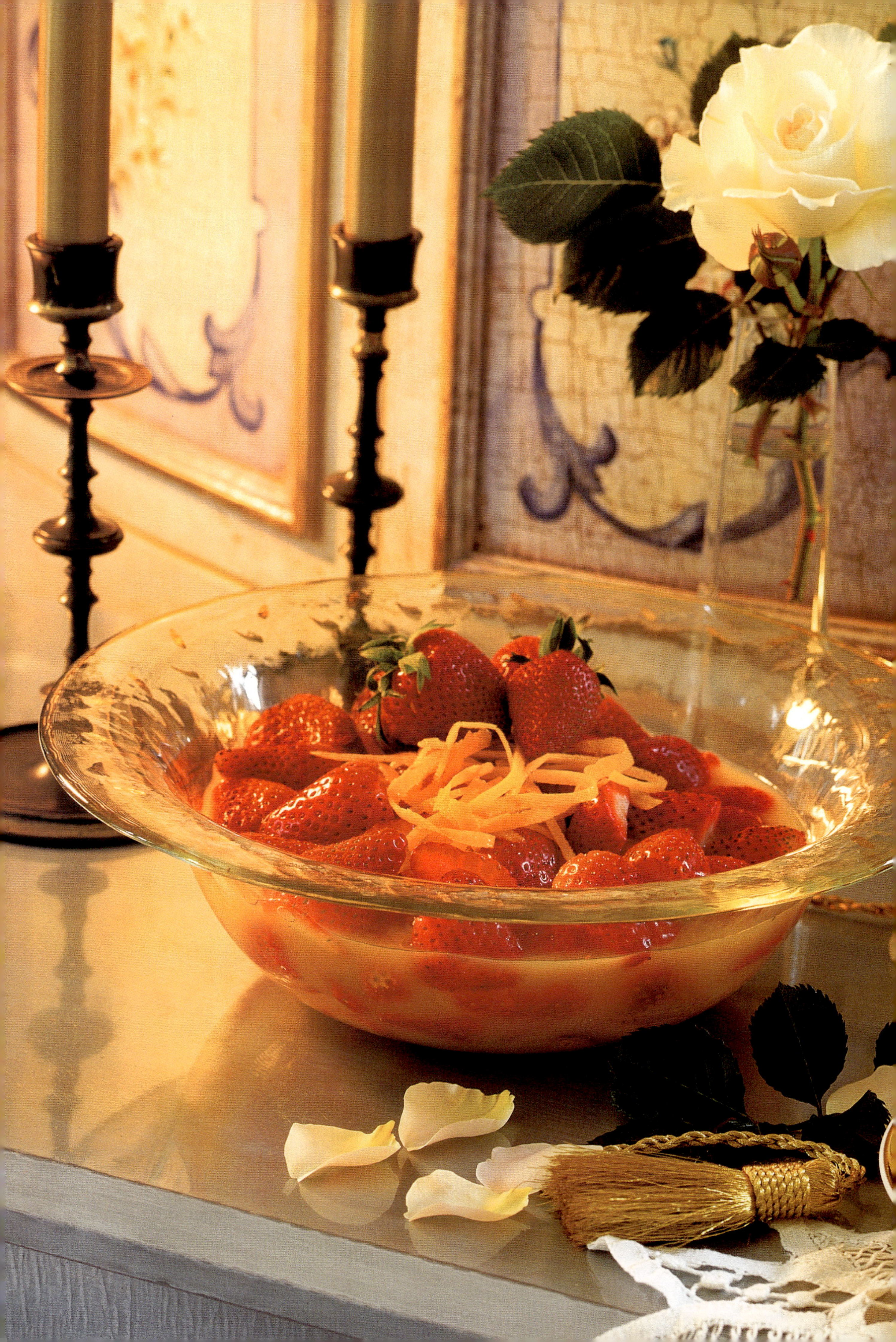

DESSERTS

COLD DESSERTS

BAKED LEMON CHEESECAKE

125 g malt biscuits
50 g butter
4 eggs
250 g pot sour cream

250 g pot plain cottage cheese
4 teaspoons grated lemon rind
2 tablespoons lemon juice
½ cup caster sugar

Crush biscuits. Melt butter. Mix biscuit crumbs and butter together and press into the bottom of a 20 cm loose-bottom tin lined on the base with baking paper. Bake at 180°C for 10 minutes. Place eggs, sour cream, cottage cheese, lemon rind, lemon juice and caster sugar in a food processor or blender and process until smooth. Pour into cooked base. Bake at 150°C for 1 hour or until cheesecake is set. Serve warm or cold. **Serves 6.** *(Pictured below left.)*

CASSATA

1 litre chocolate ice cream
½ teaspoon vanilla essence
300 ml cream
2 tablespoons icing sugar

½ cup toasted almonds
½ cup chopped dark chocolate
1 cup chopped glacé fruit

Soften ice cream and mix in vanilla essence. Use to line the base and sides of a 1 litre pudding basin. Freeze until firm. Whip cream until stiff. Fold in icing sugar, almonds, chocolate and glacé fruit. Use to fill the chocolate ice cream cavity. Cover with foil and freeze until firm. Unmould onto a serving plate by dipping bowl into hot water two to three times, then inverting onto a plate and shaking sharply. Cut into wedges to serve. **Serves 6 – 8.**

CHILLED CHEESECAKE

BASE
250 g packet Digestive biscuits
1 teaspoon grated lemon rind
1 tablespoon lemon juice
75 g butter, melted

FILLING
2 teaspoons gelatine
2 tablespoons water
250 g pot cream cheese
250 g pot sour cream
½ cup sugar
2 tablespoons lemon juice
1 teaspoon grated lemon rind
1 teaspoon vanilla essence

BASE
Finely crush biscuits. Combine biscuit crumbs, lemon rind, juice and butter. Line the base and sides of a 20 cm spring-form tin with biscuit mixture. Chill while preparing filling. Pour filling into prepared base. Chill until set. **Serves 6.**

FILLING
Combine gelatine and water. Leave to swell for 10 minutes. Beat cream cheese until soft. Add sour cream and beat until well combined. Add sugar, lemon juice, rind and vanilla. Beat until sugar has dissolved. Dissolve gelatine over hot water. Stir through cheese mixture.

EASY CHOCOLATE MOUSSE

150 g cooking chocolate
4 eggs, separated
300 ml cream

2 tablespoons sugar
whipped cream
grated chocolate

Break chocolate into the top of a double boiler. Stir over hot water until chocolate has melted. Allow to cool slightly. Stir yolks into chocolate. Beat until thick and smooth. Beat cream until thick. Fold chocolate mixture into cream. Beat egg whites until stiff but not dry. Gradually add sugar, beating until thick and glossy. Fold half egg white mixture into chocolate mixture until well mixed. Repeat with remaining egg white mixture. Pour into four or six individual dishes or one large one. Chill until firm. Serve decorated with whipped cream and chocolate. *Serves 4 – 6.*
(Pictured below left.)

CHOCOLATE LIQUEUR MOUSSE
Add 1 tablespoon brandy, chocolate or coffee liqueur to melted chocolate.

CRÈME CARAMEL

3/4 cup sugar
1/2 cup water
2 cups milk

1/2 teaspoon vanilla essence
4 eggs
2 tablespoons sugar

Combine first measure of sugar and water in a heavy-based saucepan. Gently heat, stirring constantly until sugar has dissolved. Bring to the boil. Do not stir. Leave syrup to boil until golden. Divide syrup evenly among six individual ramekin dishes. Set aside. Heat milk until almost boiling. Remove from heat. Add vanilla. In a separate bowl beat eggs and second measure of sugar together until pale. Pour heated milk onto egg mixture. Stir to combine. Strain. Divide egg mixture evenly among the caramel-lined dishes. Place dishes in a roasting dish. Pour in enough water to come halfway up the sides of ramekin dishes. Bake at 180°C for 35 minutes or until custard is set. Remove from roasting dish and allow to cool. Chill overnight then unmould onto serving plates. *Serves 6.*

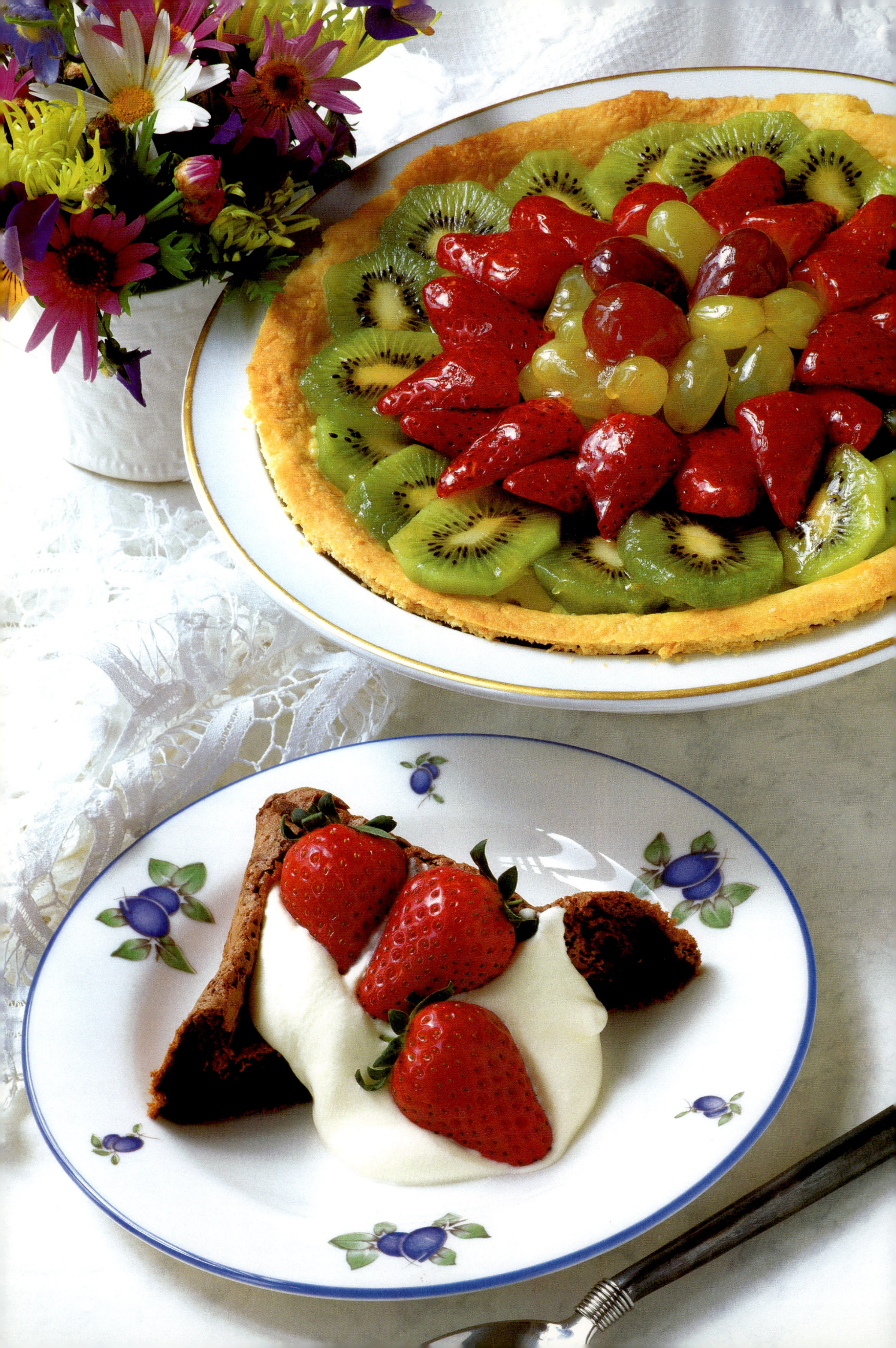

FLOURLESS CHOCOLATE CAKE

125 g cooking chocolate
50 g butter
4 eggs
3/4 cup caster sugar
1 teaspoon Edmonds
   baking powder

icing sugar
lightly whipped cream
fresh seasonal fruit

Melt chocolate and butter together over hot water or in the microwave. Separate eggs. Beat yolks and sugar together until thick and creamy. Beat egg whites until stiff peaks form. Fold melted chocolate mixture, egg yolks, egg whites and baking powder together. Pour mixture into a 20 cm cake tin lined on the base with baking paper. Bake at 180°C for 25 to 30 minutes or until cake is set. Stand in tin for 10 minutes before turning onto a wire rack. The cake shrinks down as it cools. When cold dust with icing sugar and serve with lightly whipped cream and fresh seasonal fruit. *Serves 4 – 6.*

FRUIT FLAN

200 g sweet short pastry (p. 169)

FILLING

1 cup milk
2 egg yolks
2 tablespoons sugar
2 tablespoons Edmonds
   custard powder

TOPPING
Sliced fresh or canned fruit – e.g. kiwifruit, grapes, strawberries, peaches

GLAZE
1/4 cup apricot jam
2 teaspoons water

On a lightly floured board roll out pastry and use to line a 20 cm flan ring. Bake blind at 190°C for 25 minutes. Remove baking blind material and return to oven for 1 minute to dry out pastry base. Set aside until cold. When cold pour filling into prepared base. Arrange sliced fruit decoratively over custard. Spoon or brush glaze over fruit. *Serves 6.*

FILLING
In a saucepan whisk milk with yolks, sugar and custard powder to a smooth paste. Cook over a low heat, stirring until mixture thickens. Do not boil. Remove from heat, cover and leave until cold.

GLAZE
Gently heat apricot jam and water together. Strain.

ICED COFFEE

1 cup cold double strength coffee
1 cup calcium enriched
    low-fat milk
1/2 teaspoon vanilla essence

1/4 cup whipped cream
ground cinnamon
chocolate flakes

Freeze coffee in ice cube trays. When frozen, place ice cubes, milk and vanilla in a blender or food processor. Blend or process until ice cubes are ground up and mixture slushy. Pour into tall glasses. Garnish with whipped cream, cinnamon and chocolate flakes. *Serves 2.*

LEMON TART

200 g sweet short pastry (p. 169)
4 egg yolks
1/4 cup lemon juice
1 tablespoon grated lemon rind
1/2 cup caster sugar
1 cup full-cream milk

Roll pastry out on a lightly floured board to line a 20 cm pie or quiche dish. Bake blind at 200°C for 15 minutes. Remove baking blind material and cook for a further 3 minutes. Beat egg yolks, lemon juice, lemon rind and sugar until combined. Lightly beat in milk. Pour into pastry shell. Bake at 200°C for 5 minutes, then reduce temperature to 150°C and cook for a further 20 minutes or until tart is set. Serve warm or cold. *Serves 4.*

LEMON YOGHURT ICE CREAM TERRINE

500 ml vanilla ice cream
500 g natural unsweetened
    yoghurt

1/4 cup lemon curd
1 teaspoon grated lemon rind
lemon slices

Soften ice cream. Mix yoghurt, lemon curd and lemon rind together. Mix into softened ice cream. Line a 10 x 17 cm loaf tin with foil to cover base and long sides, not ends. Spoon mixture into prepared tin. Smooth surface. Cover with foil and freeze until firm. To serve, turn onto a serving plate. Garnish with lemon slices. *Serves 4 – 6.*

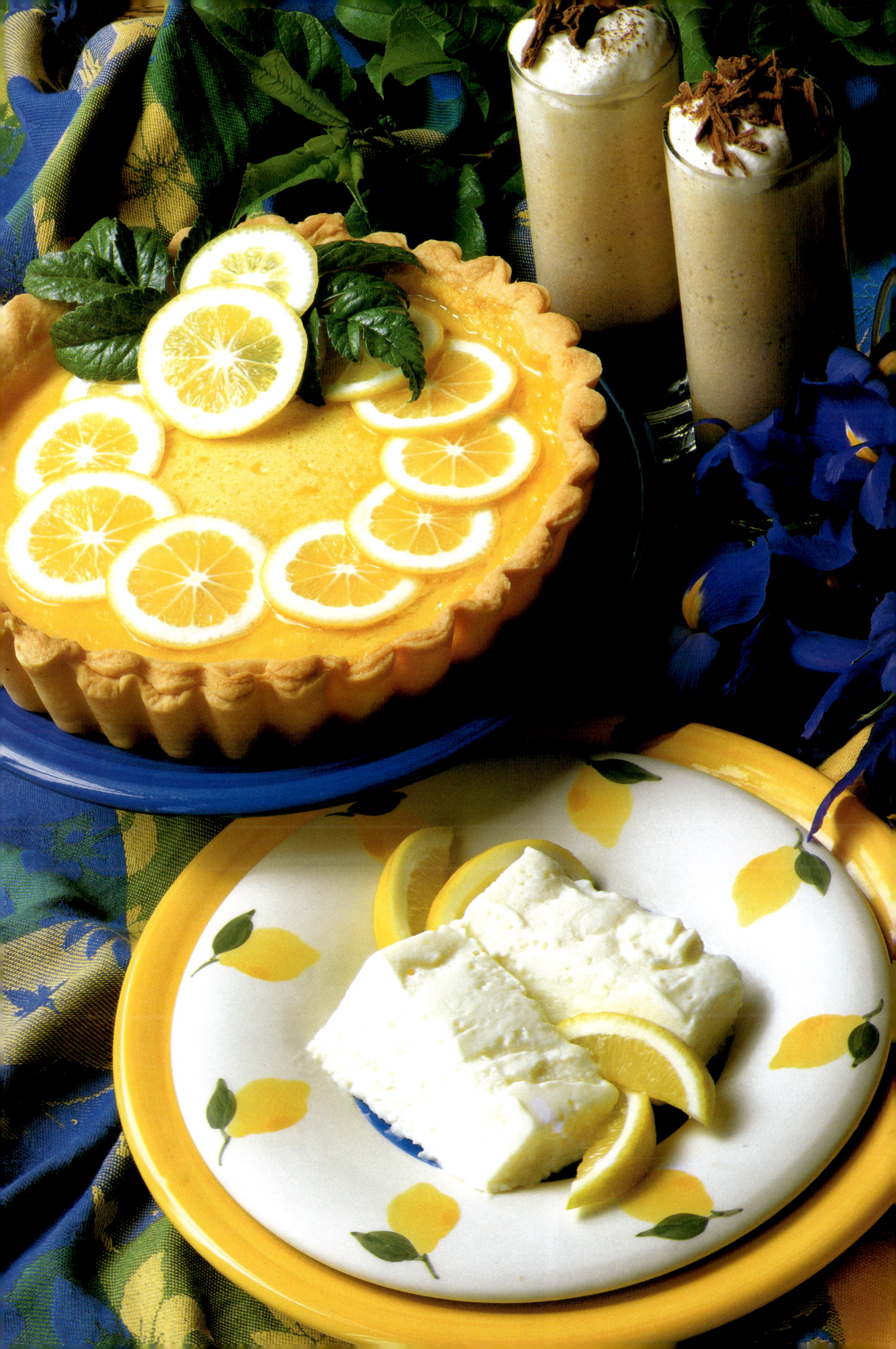

ORANGE-MARINATED STRAWBERRIES

¼ cup thinly pared orange rind
1 cup orange juice

¼ cup sugar
1 large chip or 400 g strawberries

Cut orange rind into thin strips. Place orange rind, juice and sugar in a saucepan. Bring to the boil and simmer for 5 minutes. Leave to cool. Hull strawberries and cut in half. Place in a bowl. Pour over orange mixture. Leave to marinate for 2 hours at room temperature or overnight in the refrigerator, mixing regularly. Serve lightly chilled. **Serves 4.** *(Pictured below left.)*

PLUM AND PORT JELLY

1 tablespoon gelatine
½ cup port
1 ½ cups plum juice

plums
whipped cream

Sprinkle gelatine over port and leave for 5 minutes to swell. Stand over hot water and stir until dissolved. Mix gelatine mixture into plum juice. Rinse a 2 cup jelly mould with water. Do not dry. Pour plum mixture into mould. Refrigerate until set. To unmould, quickly dip mould into hot water three times. Turn onto a serving plate and shake firmly to break the vacuum. Serve with plums or other sliced fruit and lightly whipped cream. **Serves 4.**

PAVLOVA

4 egg whites
1 1/2 cups caster sugar
1 teaspoon DYC white vinegar
1 teaspoon vanilla essence

1 tablespoon Edmonds
    Fielder's cornflour
whipped cream
fresh fruit to garnish

Preheat oven to 180°C. Using an electric mixer, beat egg whites and sugar for 10 to 15 minutes or until thick and glossy. Mix vinegar, vanilla and cornflour together. Add to meringue. Beat on high speed for a further 5 minutes. Line an oven tray with baking paper. Draw a 22 cm circle on the baking paper. Spread the pavlova mixture to within 2 cm of the edge of the circle, keeping the shape as round and even as possible. Smooth top surface over. Place pavlova in preheated oven then turn oven temperature down to 100°C. Bake pavlova for 1 hour. Turn oven off. Open oven door slightly and leave pavlova in oven until cold. Carefully lift pavlova onto a serving plate. Decorate with whipped cream and fresh fruit. **Serves 6.**

SHERRY TRIFLE

200 g packet trifle sponge
¼ cup raspberry or apricot jam
¼ cup sherry
410 g can fruit salad
4 tablespoons Edmonds
   custard powder
3 tablespoons sugar

2 cups milk
2 egg whites
300 ml cream
½ teaspoon vanilla essence
1 tablespoon icing sugar
¼ cup chopped nuts

Cut sponge in half horizontally. Spread cut surface with jam. Sandwich halves together. Cut into cubes then put into serving dish. Spoon sherry over sponge. Spoon fruit salad and juice evenly over sponge. Set aside. Mix custard powder, sugar and ½ a cup of measured milk in a saucepan. Stir in remaining milk. Heat to boiling, then simmer for 2 to 3 minutes or until thickened. Stir constantly. Remove from heat. Cover and leave until cool. When custard has cooled, beat egg whites until stiff. Fold custard into egg whites. Pour custard over fruit salad in serving dish. Chill until set. Beat cream until thick. Stir in vanilla and icing sugar. Decorate trifle with cream and nuts. *Serves 6 – 8.* *(Pictured below left.)*

SORBET

500 g fruit – e.g. grapes,
   boysenberries, plums,
   strawberries, blueberries
½ cup sugar

1 cup water
¼ cup lemon juice
2 egg whites

Purée fruit to be used. Strain and discard the skins and seeds. Set aside. In a saucepan, combine sugar and water. Cook over a low heat, stirring constantly until sugar has dissolved. Remove from heat and allow to cool slightly. Combine sugar syrup, fruit purée and lemon juice. Pour into a shallow container. Put in freezer until mixture starts to freeze on top. Transfer mixture to a bowl. Add egg whites and beat until combined. Refreeze until set. Serve in chilled glasses. *Serves 6.*

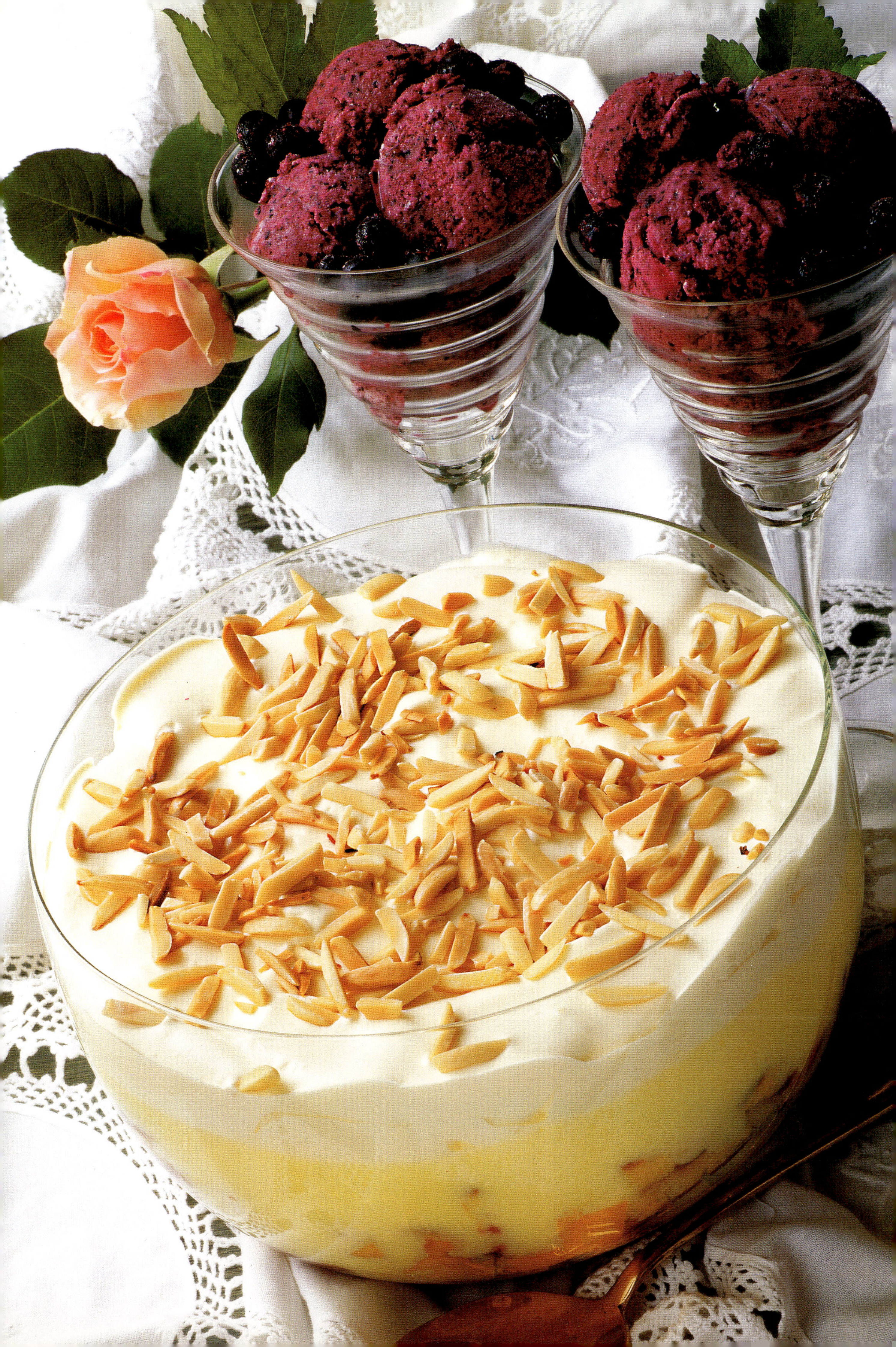

SUMMER BERRIES WITH PRALINE AND CUSTARD

2 tablespoons Edmonds
    custard powder
1 teaspoon sugar
1 cup milk
300 ml cream

3 cups mixed fresh berries such as
    strawberries, raspberries,
    boysenberries and blueberries

PRALINE
1/2 cup roasted almonds
1/2 cup sugar

Mix custard powder and sugar with 1/4 cup of the measured milk in a saucepan. Stir in remaining milk. Heat to boiling then simmer for 2 to 3 minutes or until thickened. Stir constantly. Cover surface of custard with baking paper. Leave until cold. Whip cream until soft. Fold cream and custard together. Pile berries on a platter or in a bowl. Pour over custard mixture. Garnish with shards of praline. *Serves 4.* (Pictured below left.)

PRALINE

Spread almonds on a baking tray. Gently heat sugar in a heavy frying pan until it starts to melt. Continue to heat until sugar starts to turn golden. Do not stir. Remove from heat. Pour over nuts on tray in a thin layer. Leave until hard and break into shards.

SUMMER PUDDING

5 cups mixed berry fruit
1 1/4 cups sugar
10 slices stale bread

Prepare fruit, washing, drying, hulling and slicing if large. Mix fruit and sugar together and heat gently until almost boiling. Remove from heat and cool. Cut crusts from bread and cut each slice into 3 fingers. Arrange bread around the inside of a 6-cup pudding basin. Spoon in one-third of the berry mixture. Layer with more bread then repeat, finishing with a layer of bread. Spoon over enough berry juice to moisten bread. Cover with plastic wrap and weigh down with a heavy weight. Refrigerate for 2 hours or overnight. Turn onto a serving plate and serve cut into wedges. *Serves 6 – 8.*

TIRAMISÙ

1/4 cup Edmonds custard powder
2 tablespoons sugar
2 1/2 cups milk
125 g packet sponge fingers
1/4 cup triple strength coffee
1/4 cup brandy
250 g pot low fat sour cream
whipped cream
1/4 cup grated chocolate

Mix custard powder and sugar with 1/2 a cup of the measured milk in a saucepan. Stir in remaining milk. Heat to boiling then simmer for 2 to 3 minutes or until thickened. Stir constantly. Cover surface with baking paper and leave until cold. Arrange sponge fingers over the base and sides of a serving bowl. Mix coffee and brandy together. Pour over sponge fingers. Mix sour cream into custard. Spoon over sponge fingers. Garnish with whipped cream and grated chocolate. *Serves 6 – 8.*

HOT PUDDINGS

APPLE PIE

200 g sweet shortcrust pastry (p.169)
25 g butter, melted
milk or water
2 teaspoons sugar

FILLING
4 to 6 granny smith apples
½ cup sugar
2 tablespoons Champion standard
   plain flour
¼ teaspoon ground cloves

On a lightly floured board roll out pastry slightly larger than a 20 cm pie plate. Cut two 2.5 cm wide strips long enough to go around the edge of the pie plate. Brush with water. Spoon apple filling into centre of pie plate. Pour butter over filling. Cover with remaining pastry. Press edges firmly together to seal. Cut steam holes in centre of pastry. Trim and crimp edges. Decorate pie with any pastry trimmings. Brush lightly with milk or water. Sprinkle with sugar. Bake at 200°C for 25 minutes or until pastry is golden. Test with a skewer if the apple is cooked. If not, reduce oven temperature to 180°C and cook until apple is tender. **Serves 6.** *(Pictured below left.)*

FILLING
Peel, core and slice the apples. Combine sugar, flour and cloves. Toss apples in this mixture.

APPLE STRUDEL

6 sheets filo pastry
½ cup soft breadcrumbs
567 g can spiced apples

½ cup sultanas
1 tablespoon melted butter
icing sugar

Place filo sheets under a damp tea-towel. Sprinkle breadcrumbs between each sheet, layering as you go on a greased oven tray. Mix apples and sultanas together. Spread over half of the pastry to within 5 cm from edge. Wet pastry edges. Fold pastry over filling and seal edges. Cut three slashes in top of pastry. Brush with butter. Bake at 200°C for 25 minutes or until pastry is golden. Dust with icing sugar and serve warm or cold. **Serves 4.**

BREAD AND BUTTER PUDDING

4 x 2 cm thick slices stale
   spiced fruit loaf
4 eggs
1 cup full-cream milk

½ cup cream
1 teaspoon grated lemon rind
icing sugar

Cut bread into quarters and arrange over the base of an ovenproof dish. Beat eggs, milk, cream and lemon rind together until combined. Pour through a sieve over bread. Bake in a bain marie at 180°C for 30 to 35 minutes or until set. Serve dusted with icing sugar. *Serves 6.*

CHOCOLATE SELF-SAUCING PUDDING

100 g butter, softened
¾ cup sugar
1 egg
1 teaspoon vanilla essence
1 ¼ cups Champion standard
   plain flour
2 teaspoons Edmonds
   baking powder

1 tablespoon cocoa
2 cups boiling water

SAUCE
½ cup brown sugar
1 tablespoon Edmonds Fielder's
   cornflour
2 tablespoons cocoa

Beat butter, sugar, egg and vanilla together. Sift flour, baking powder and cocoa together. Fold into beaten mixture. Spoon mixture into a greased ovenproof dish. Sprinkle sauce mixture over. Carefully pour boiling water over the back of a spoon onto the pudding. Bake at 180°C for 35 minutes or until pudding springs back when lightly touched. *Serves 6.*

SAUCE
Combine all ingredients.

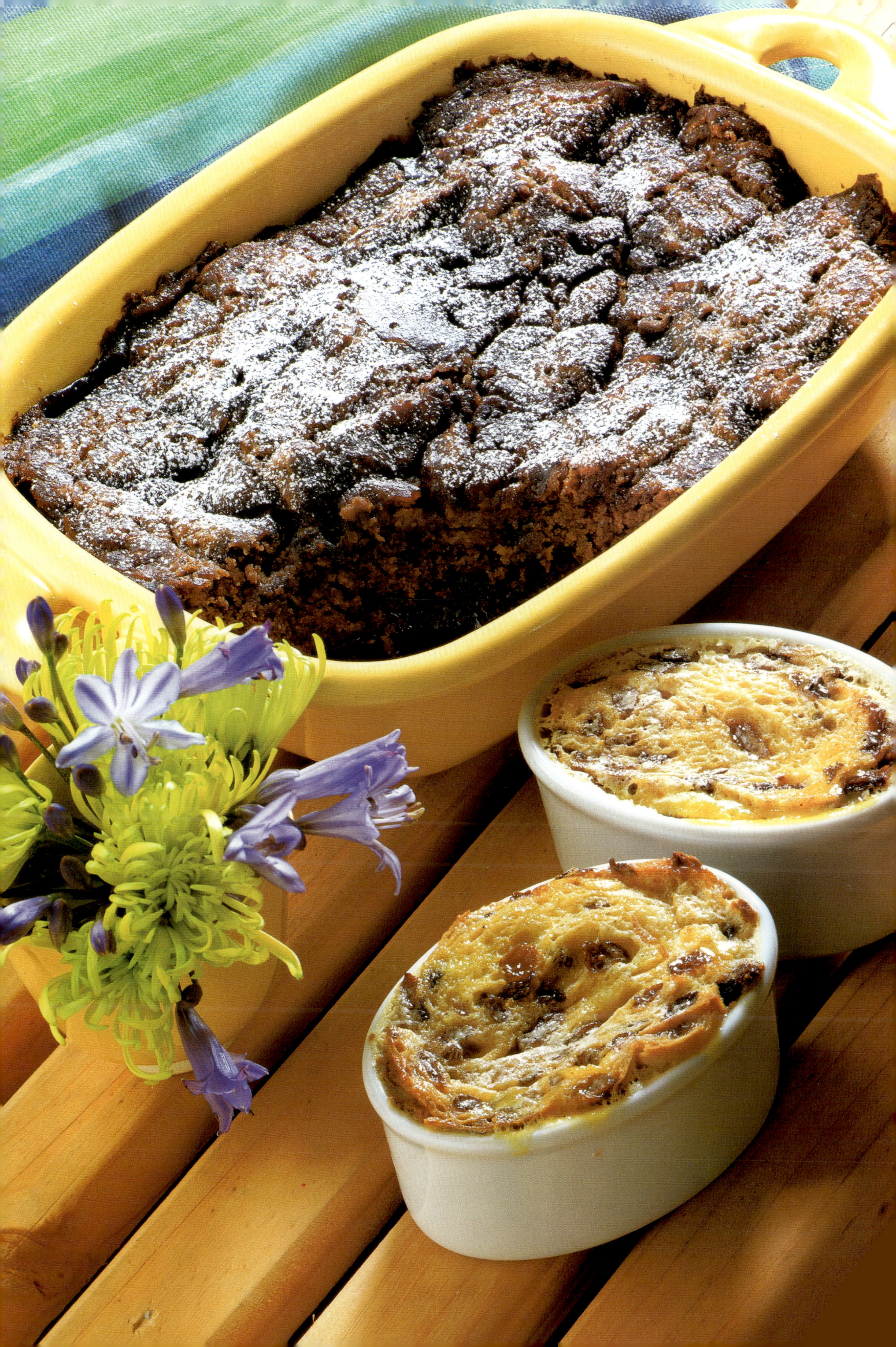

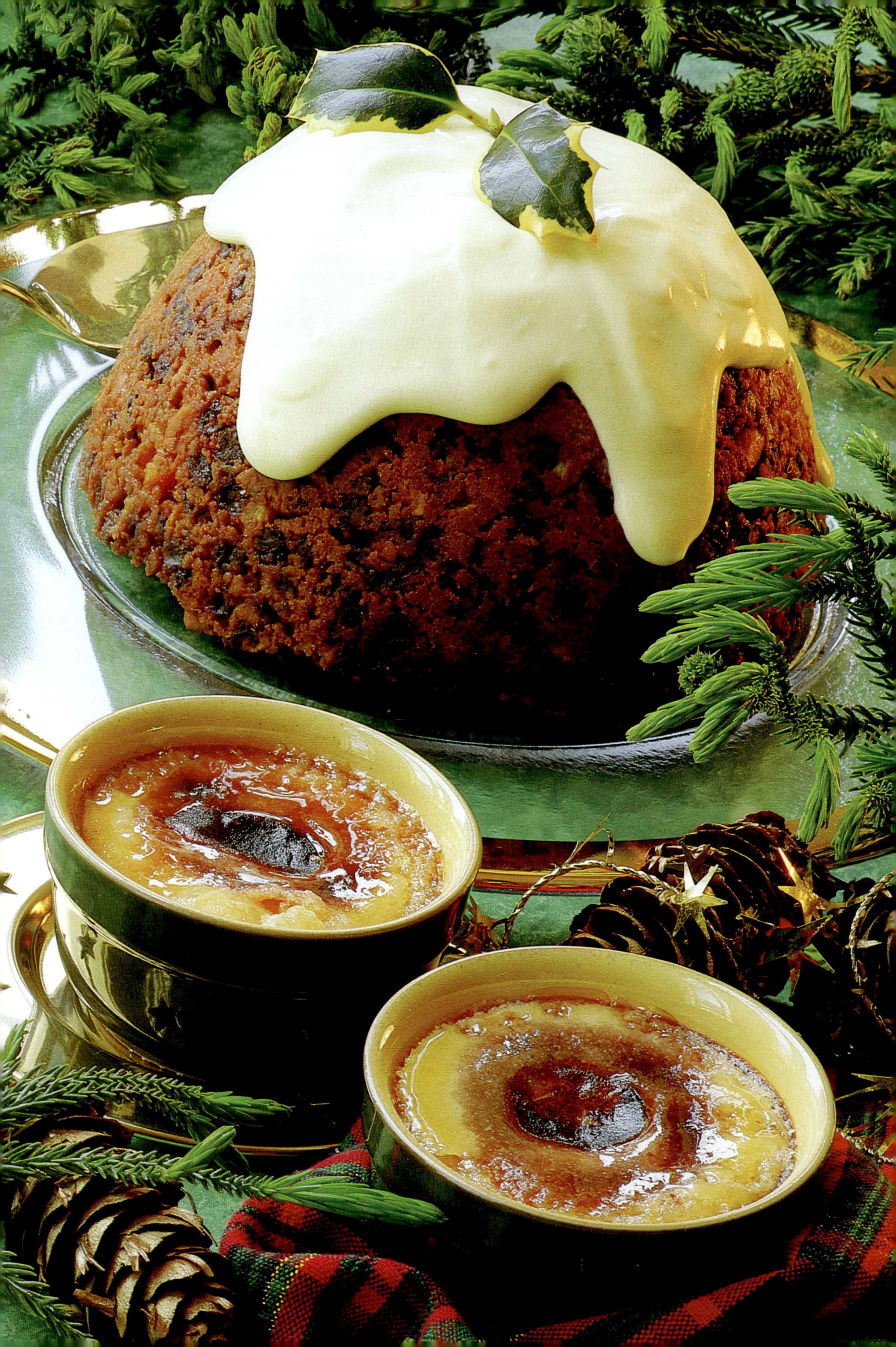

CHRISTMAS PUDDING

1 cup sultanas
1 cup raisins
1 cup currants
70 g packet blanched almonds, chopped
150 g packet mixed peel
1 cup shredded suet
1 cup Champion standard plain flour
1½ teaspoons Edmonds baking powder
1 teaspoon mixed spice
1 teaspoon cinnamon
¼ teaspoon ground nutmeg
¼ teaspoon salt
1½ cups soft breadcrumbs
1 cup brown sugar
2 eggs
2 teaspoons grated lemon rind
½ cup milk
1 tablespoon brandy

Put sultanas, raisins, currants, almonds and mixed peel into a large bowl. Add suet, mixing to combine. Sift flour, baking powder, mixed spice, cinnamon, nutmeg and salt into fruit mixture. Mix well. Add breadcrumbs and mix through. In a separate bowl beat brown sugar, eggs, lemon rind and milk together. Add to fruit mixture, mixing thoroughly to combine. Stir in brandy. Spoon mixture into a well-greased six-cup-capacity pudding basin. Cover with pleated greaseproof paper or foil. Secure with string, leaving a loop to lift out pudding when cooked. Place a trivet or old saucer in the bottom of a large saucepan half-filled with boiling water. Carefully lower pudding into saucepan, making sure the water comes two-thirds of the way up the sides of basin. Cover and cook for 5 hours, making sure water is constantly bubbling. Check water level from time to time. Remove from saucepan. Leave until cold. Wrap well and store in refrigerator until ready to use. Steam for a further 2 hours before serving. **Serves 6.** *(Pictured below left.)*

CRÈME BRÛLÉE

4 egg yolks
2 eggs
¼ cup caster sugar
½ teaspoon vanilla essence
1 cup cream
1 cup sugar

Beat egg yolks, eggs, caster sugar and vanilla together until combined. Mix in cream. Pour into 4 individual ½-cup ramekins and bake in a bain marie at 160°C for 25 minutes or until brûlées are almost set. Alternatively cook in a 3-cup capacity ovenproof dish. Remove from oven and leave to cool and firm. Sprinkle sugar over ramekins. Grill slowly until sugar is melted and golden. Serve immediately. **Serves 4.**

FRUIT CRUMBLE

2 cups stewed fruit – e.g. apples,
    plums, apricots
2 tablespoons brown sugar
1 cup Champion standard
    plain flour
1 teaspoon Edmonds
    baking powder
50 g butter
¼ cup sugar

Place stewed fruit in bottom of an ovenproof dish. Sprinkle with brown sugar. Sift flour and baking powder into a bowl. Cut in butter until mixture resembles coarse breadcrumbs. Stir in sugar. Spoon mixture over fruit. Bake at 190°C for 30 minutes or until pale golden. *Serves 6.*
(Main picture, bottom.)

WHOLEMEAL CRUMBLE
Replace flour with Champion wholemeal flour. Increase butter to 75 g.

WHOLEGRAIN OAT CRUMBLE
Reduce flour to ½ cup. Increase butter to 75 g. Stir in ½ cup Fleming's wholegrain oats after sugar.

FRUIT BETTY
Omit flour and baking powder and replace with 2 cups soft breadcrumbs. Increase butter to 100 g and melt. Combine butter and breadcrumbs, cooking until pale golden and slightly crisp. Add remaining crumble ingredients. Layer apple mixture with breadcrumb mixture, finishing with a layer of breadcrumbs. Cook as above until golden.

LEMON MERINGUE PIE

BASE
200 g sweet shortcrust pastry (p. 169)

FILLING
¼ cup Edmonds Fielder's
    cornflour
2 tablespoons Edmonds
    custard powder
1 cup sugar
2 teaspoons grated lemon rind
¼ cup lemon juice
¾ cup water
3 eggs, separated
1 tablespoon butter

TOPPING
¼ cup caster sugar
¼ teaspoon vanilla essence

On a lightly floured board roll out pastry to 6 mm thickness. Use to line a 20 cm flan ring. Trim off any excess pastry. Bake blind at 190°C for 20 minutes. Remove baking blind material. Return pastry shell to oven for 1 minute to dry out pastry base. While pastry is cooking make the filling. Pour filling into cooked pastry base. Spoon meringue topping over lemon filling. Return to oven and bake at 190°C for 10 minutes or until golden. *Serves 6.*

FILLING
Blend cornflour, custard powder, sugar, lemon rind and juice together until smooth. Add water. Cook over medium heat until mixture boils and thickens, stirring constantly. Remove from heat. Stir in yolks and butter.

TOPPING
Beat egg whites until stiff but not dry. Beat in sugar, 1 tablespoon at a time, until very thick and glossy. Stir in vanilla.

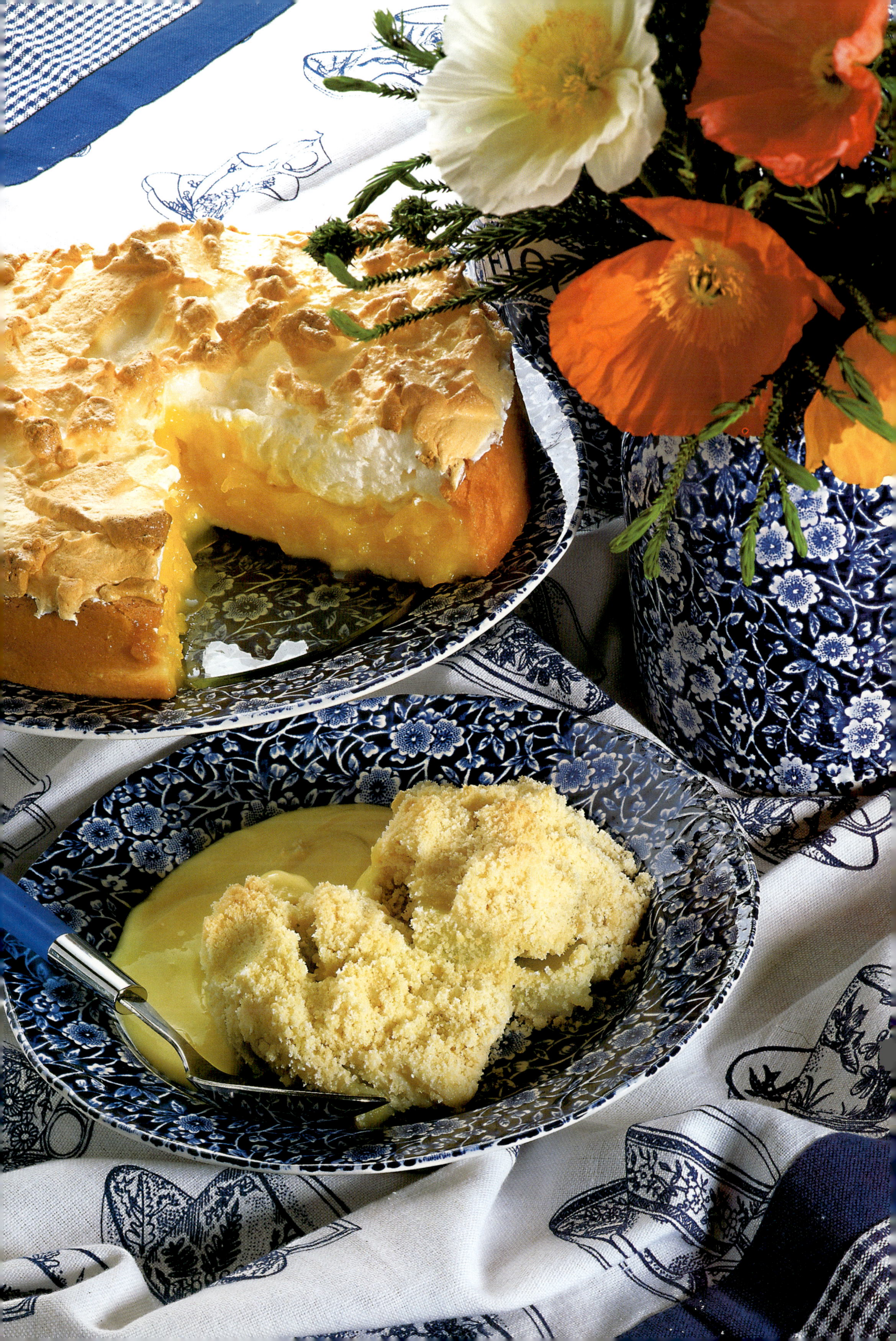

PEAR TARTE TATIN

820 g can pear halves
50 g butter

1 cup sugar
2 sheets pre-rolled flaky pastry

Drain pears. Melt butter and sugar in a frying pan about 20 cm in diameter and with a metal handle. Arrange pears in a cartwheel fashion in the pan. Brush one pastry sheet lightly with water and place second sheet on top of first. Cut pastry to the same diameter as the frying pan used. Place pastry over pears and cook over a medium heat for 15 minutes. Remove from heat and place pan in oven. Bake at 220°C for 10 to 15 minutes or until pastry is golden. Turn onto a serving plate and serve hot. *Serves 4 – 6.*

PECAN PIE

200 g sweet shortcrust pastry (p. 169)

FILLING
100 g butter, softened
½ cup brown sugar
3 eggs
3 tablespoons liquid honey
3 x 70 g packets pecan nuts

On a lightly floured board roll out pastry and use to line a 22 cm flan tin. Bake blind at 200°C for 15 minutes. Remove baking blind material. Return pastry shell to oven for 1 minute to dry out pastry base. Reduce oven temperature to 180°C. Pour filling into cooked pastry base. Return to oven and bake for a further 30 minutes or until filling is set. **Serves 6.** *(Pictured below left.)*

FILLING
Cream butter and sugar until light and fluffy. Add eggs one at a time, beating well after each addition. Stir in honey and pecans.

STICKY DATE PUDDING WITH CARAMEL SAUCE

2 cups pitted dates
¼ cup brown sugar
½ cup boiling water
½ teaspoon baking soda
150 g butter
1 cup sugar
3 eggs
3 cups Champion standard plain flour
3 teaspoons Edmonds baking powder
caramel sauce

Chop dates roughly. Place in a saucepan with brown sugar, water and baking soda. Set aside. Melt butter in a saucepan large enough to mix all ingredients. Mix in sugar. Beat eggs and add to saucepan with flour, baking powder and date mixture. Mix to combine. Pour into a 20 cm square cake tin or ovenproof dish lined on the bottom with baking paper. Bake at 180°C for 45 minutes or until pudding springs back when lightly touched. Serve with ready-made hot caramel sauce. **Serves 4 – 6.**

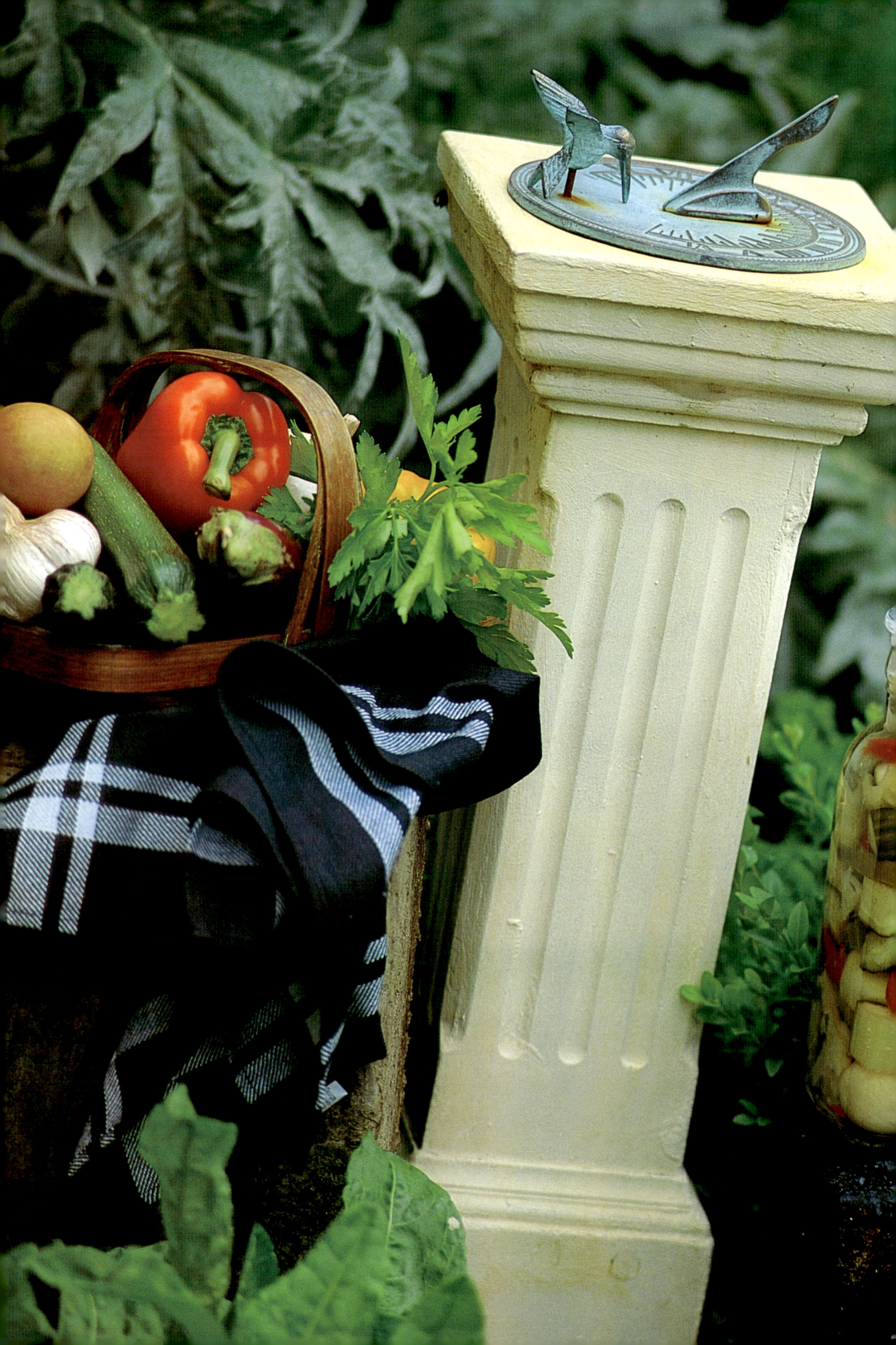

PRESERVES

PRESERVES

APRICOT JAM

2.75 kg apricots, halved and stoned
10 to 12 apricot kernels
2 1/2 cups water
12 cups sugar

Crack a few apricot stones and remove kernels. Put apricots, kernels and water into a preserving pan. Cook slowly until fruit is pulpy. Add sugar. Stir until dissolved. Boil briskly for 30 minutes or until setting point is reached. Pour into hot, clean, dry jars. *Makes about 10 x 350 ml jars.*
(Main picture, top left.)

FETTA AND OLIVE PRESERVE

2 stems rosemary about 8 cm long
1/4 cup dry sundried tomatoes
300 g fetta cheese
4 shallots
1 cup black olives
about 2 cups olive oil

Blanch the rosemary and sundried tomatoes in boiling water for 1 minute. Dry in a 180°C oven for 5 minutes. Cut rosemary into 4 cm lengths. Cut fetta into 1 cm cubes. Peel shallots and cut into thin slices. Layer fetta cheese, olives, shallot slices and sundried tomatoes into clean, dry jars. Add rosemary pieces and pour over enough olive oil to cover the cheese. Seal and store in the refrigerator for at least 2 weeks before using. Use the oil for cooking or making dressings and eat the cheese and olive mixture with crusty bread or as part of an antipasto platter. *Makes 3 cups.*

INDIAN MANGO CHUTNEY

2 limes
salt
425 g can mango slices
2 onions
4 cloves garlic
1 tablespoon hot curry powder
2 tablespoons finely chopped root ginger
2 cups DYC white vinegar
3/4 cup brown sugar

Cut limes into eighths and sprinkle with salt. Leave for 1 hour. Rinse limes and dry. Drain mango slices. Peel onions and chop coarsely. Crush, peel and chop garlic. Place mango slices, limes, onions, garlic, curry powder, ginger, vinegar and brown sugar into a preserving pan. Cook mixture over a medium heat for 1 hour or until mixture is thick and pulpy. Spoon into hot, clean, dry jars. Seal when cold. *Makes about 3 cups.*

LEMON HONEY

50 g butter
3/4 cup sugar
1 cup lemon juice (see p. 171)
2 eggs, beaten
1 teaspoon finely grated
    lemon rind

Melt the butter in the top of a double boiler. Stir in sugar and lemon juice until sugar is dissolved. Add eggs and lemon rind. Place over boiling water and cook, stirring all the time until mixture thickens. Pour into hot, clean, dry jars. **Makes about 2 x 250 ml jars.**

MARMALADE

4 large grapefruit, minced,
    chopped or thinly sliced
2 lemons, minced, chopped or
    thinly sliced
3.4 litres water
sugar

Cover grapefruit and lemons with water and stand overnight. Next day boil for 45 minutes or until fruit is soft and pulpy. Allow to cool a little. Measure pulp and return to pan. Bring to the boil. For each cup of pulp, add 1 cup sugar. Stir until dissolved. Boil briskly, stirring occasionally until setting point is reached. Pour into hot, clean, dry jars. **Makes about 10 x 350 ml jars.**

PICKLED ONIONS

1.5 kg pickling onions
1/2 cup salt
water

3 dry chillies, approximately
6 peppercorns, approximately
DYC malt or white vinegar

Put onions in a non-metallic bowl. Sprinkle with salt. Add cold water to cover onions. Stand for 24 hours. Drain and rinse in cold water. Drain again and pack into jars. To each jar add 1 chilli and 2 peppercorns. Add vinegar to cover onions. Seal with non-metallic lids or corks. Store for 4 to 6 weeks before using. **Makes about 3 x 500 ml jars.** *(Main picture, top.)*

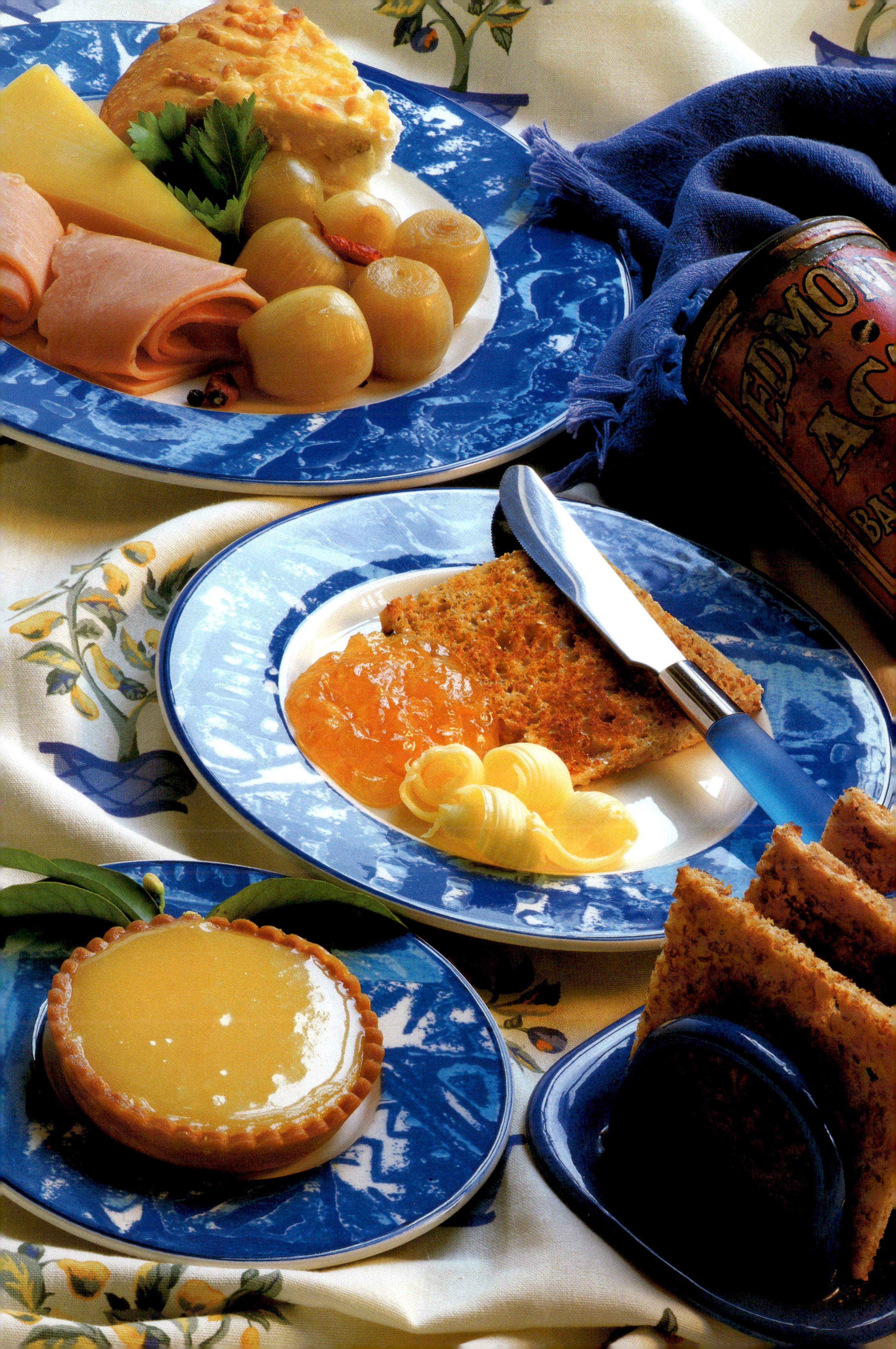

PICKLED VEGETABLES

12 shallots or pickling onions
1 cucumber, diced
1 cup sliced celery
1 cup sliced green beans
2 cups cauliflower florets

1 red pepper, sliced
6 tablespoons salt
500 ml DYC spiced vinegar,
    approximately

Prepare vegetables so pieces are of similar size. Put onions, cucumber and celery in one non-metallic bowl; the beans and cauliflower in another and the red pepper in a third. Sprinkle red pepper with 1 tablespoon salt and divide the remaining salt between the other two bowls. Cover and leave to stand for 12 hours. Next day drain off liquid formed. Rinse in cold water and drain again. Put the cauliflower and beans into a wire basket or sieve and blanch in boiling water for 2 minutes. Drain well. Mix all vegetables together and pack into hot, clean, dry jars. Pour spiced vinegar over to cover. Seal with non-metallic lids. Keep for a minimum of 3 weeks before using. *Makes about 2 x 500 ml jars.*

PLUM JAM

2 kg plums, halved and stoned
1 1/2 cups water
7 cups sugar

Put plums and water into a preserving pan. Boil until soft and pulpy. Add sugar. Stir until dissolved. Boil briskly for 15 minutes or until setting point is reached. Pour into hot, clean, dry jars. *Makes about 6 x 350 ml jars.*

PLUM SAUCE

2.75 kg plums
1.75 litres DYC malt vinegar
3 cups brown sugar
8 – 10 cloves garlic
2 teaspoons ground pepper
2 teaspoons ground cloves
2 teaspoons ground ginger
1 teaspoon ground mace
1/2 teaspoon cayenne pepper
1 tablespoon salt

Put all the ingredients into a preserving pan. Bring to the boil, stirring frequently. Boil steadily until mixture is pulpy. Press through a colander or coarse sieve. Return sauce to pan and boil for 2 to 3 minutes. Pour into hot, clean, dry bottles and seal. *Makes about 1.5 litres.*

PRESERVED LEMONS

500 g small even-sized lemons
1 cup plain salt
1 cup water
1/2 cup sugar
1 cup DYC cider vinegar
cinnamon sticks

Wash the lemons and halve crosswise. Place in a non-metallic bowl. Sprinkle over salt and leave for 2 days. Rinse lemons and dry. Pack into hot, clean, dry jars. Bring water, sugar, vinegar and cinnamon sticks to the boil and simmer for 5 minutes. Pour over lemons to cover. Clean rim of jar and seal. Lemons are sealed when the lid is concave. *Makes about 4 cups.*

KIWIFRUIT RELISH

500 g kiwifruit
1 onion
3 fresh chillies

1 tablespoon finely chopped
　fresh ginger
1 cup brown sugar
1 cup DYC cider vinegar

Peel kiwifruit and chop roughly. Peel onion and chop finely. De-seed chillies and slice finely. Place kiwifruit, onion, chillies, ginger, sugar and vinegar in a saucepan. Cook over medium heat for 50 minutes or until mixture is thick and pulpy. Pack into hot, clean, dry jars. Seal while hot. **Makes about 2 cups.** *(Main picture, top right.)*

RASPBERRY JAM

3 cups raspberries,
　fresh or frozen
2 3/4 cups sugar

Put the berries into a preserving pan and cook slowly until juice runs from them. Bring to the boil. Add sugar and stir until dissolved. Boil briskly for 3 to 5 minutes. Pour into hot, clean, dry jars. This jam firms up after a few days' storage.
Makes about 2 x 350 ml jars.

BOYSENBERRY JAM
Omit raspberries and replace with boysenberries.

STRAWBERRY JAM

1 kg strawberries, hulled
6 cups sugar
1 1/2 teaspoons tartaric acid

Put strawberries into a preserving pan. Crush lightly with a potato masher or fork. Add sugar and stir in thoroughly. Bring to the boil and boil for 5 minutes. Add tartaric acid and boil rapidly for a further 5 minutes. Pour into hot, clean, dry jars. *Makes about 3 x 350 ml jars.*

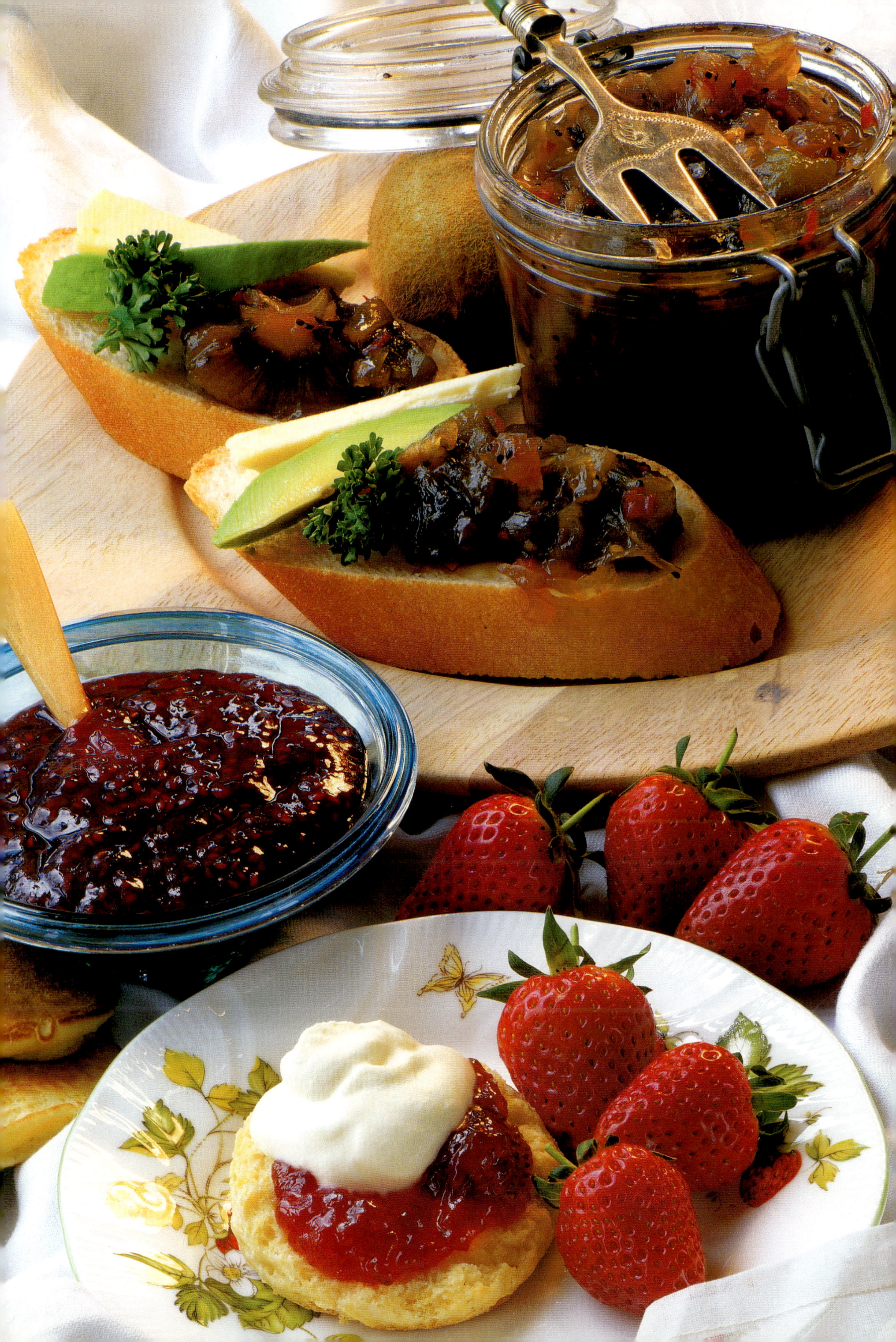

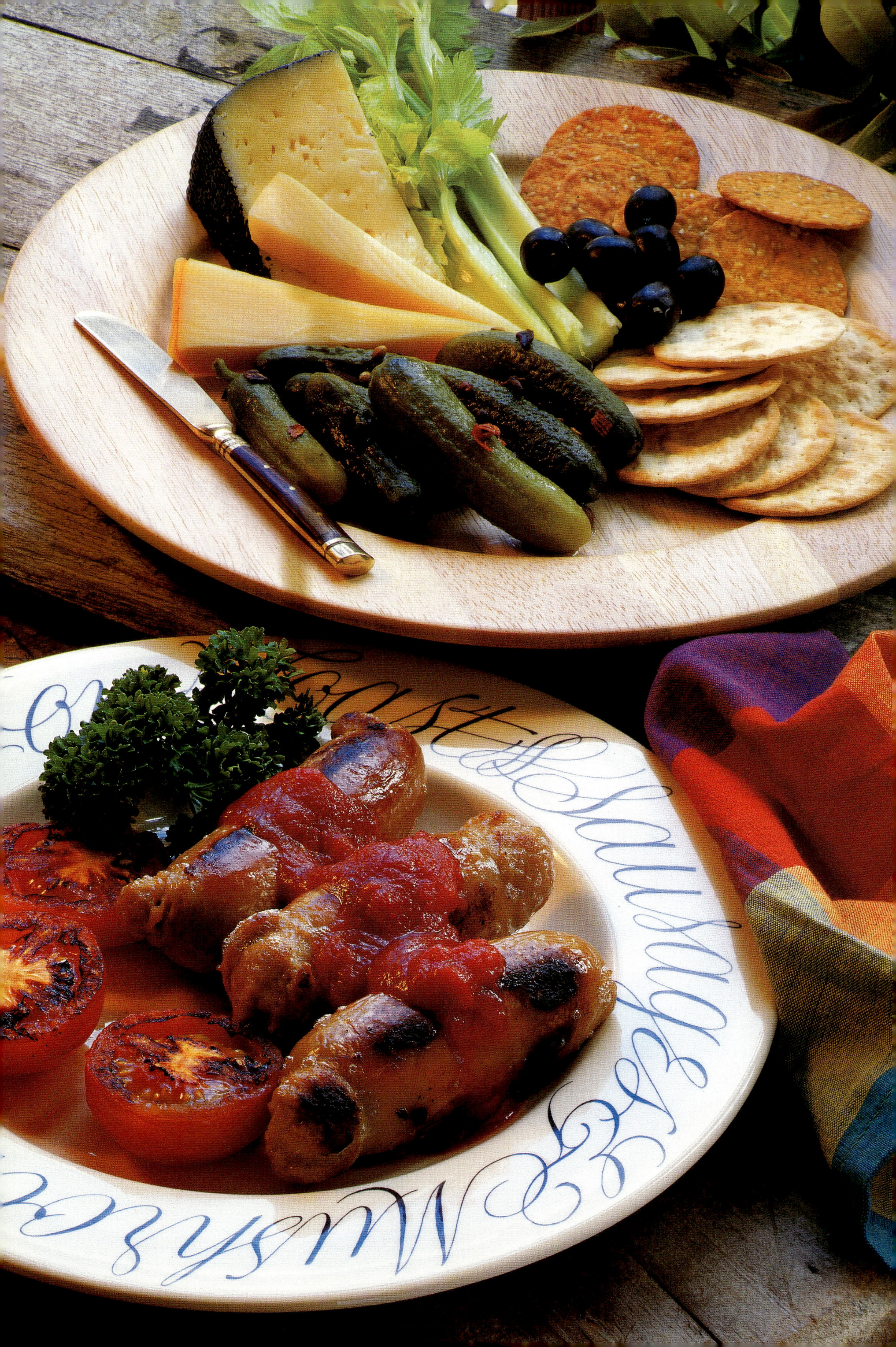
Sausage

TOMATO SAUCE

3.5 kg tomatoes, chopped
1 kg apples, peeled and chopped
6 onions, chopped
3 cups sugar
4 cups DYC malt vinegar

2 tablespoons salt
1/2 to 1 teaspoon cayenne pepper
1 teaspoon black peppercorns
1 teaspoon whole allspice
2 teaspoons whole cloves

Put tomatoes, apples, onions, sugar, vinegar, salt and cayenne pepper into a preserving pan. Tie peppercorns, allspice and cloves in muslin and add to tomato mixture. Boil steadily for about 2 hours or until completely pulpy. Discard whole spices. Press through a colander or coarse sieve. Return to pan and boil for 2 minutes. Pour into hot, clean, dry bottles and seal.
Makes about 1.75 litres.

SWEET PICKLED GHERKINS

4 kg gherkins
1/2 cup salt
6 cups water
2.25 litres DYC malt vinegar

5 cups brown sugar
25 g whole mixed pickling spice
10 cm piece cinnamon stick
1 teaspoon whole cloves

Using a piece of coarse cloth or sugar sack, rub the gherkins to remove any roughness. In a non-metallic bowl mix salt and water together. Add gherkins. Leave to soak for 24 hours. Next day combine vinegar, sugar, pickling spice, cinnamon and cloves and boil for 5 minutes. Drain gherkins and pour boiling water over to completely cover. Drain. Pack while still hot into hot, clean, dry jars. Pour hot vinegar mixture over to cover gherkins. Seal at once with non-metallic lids. Keep for a minimum of 3 weeks before using. *Makes about 6 x 500 ml jars.*

ICINGS, CUSTARD, PASTRIES, DRESSINGS & SAUCES

BUTTER ICING

100 g butter, softened
1/4 teaspoon vanilla essence
2 cups icing sugar, sifted
1 to 2 tablespoons hot water

Cream butter until light and fluffy. Add vanilla. Gradually beat in icing sugar, beating until smooth. Add sufficient water to give a spreading consistency.

CREAM CHEESE ICING

2 tablespoons butter, softened
1/4 cup cream cheese
1 cup icing sugar
1/2 teaspoon grated lemon rind

Beat butter and cream cheese until creamy. Mix in icing sugar and lemon rind, beating well to combine.

WHITE ICING

2 cups icing sugar
1/4 teaspoon butter
2 tablespoons water, approximately
1/4 teaspoon vanilla essence

Sift icing sugar into a bowl. Add butter. Add sufficient water to mix to a spreadable consistency. Flavour with vanilla essence.

CHOCOLATE ICING

Sift 1 tablespoon cocoa with the icing sugar.

COFFEE ICING

Dissolve 2 teaspoons instant coffee in 1 tablespoon hot water. Mix into icing sugar.

LEMON ICING

Replace vanilla with 1 teaspoon grated lemon rind. Replace water with lemon juice. Add a few drops of yellow food colouring if wished.

ORANGE ICING

Replace vanilla with 2 teaspoons grated orange rind. Replace water with orange juice. Add a few drops of yellow and red food colouring if wished.

PINK ICING

Add 2 drops of red food colouring.

EDMONDS CUSTARD

Conventional Method

Mix 2 tablespoons custard powder and 1 tablespoon sugar with 1/4 cup milk in a saucepan. Stir 1 3/4 cups milk into the custard mixture. Heat to boiling, then simmer for 2 to 3 minutes or until thickened. Stir constantly. Serve immediately or cool quickly by standing the saucepan in cold water.

Microwave Method

Mix 2 tablespoons custard powder and 1 tablespoon sugar with 1/4 cup milk in a large microwave safe jug or bowl. Stir 1 3/4 cups milk into the custard mixture. Cook on high (100%) power for 5 to 6 minutes or until thickened, stirring well after each minute. Serve immediately or cool quickly by standing the jug or bowl in cold water.

FLAKY PASTRY

2 cups Champion high grade flour
1/4 teaspoon salt
200 g butter
6 tablespoons cold water, approximately

Sift flour and salt into a bowl. Cut one-quarter of the butter into the flour until it resembles fine breadcrumbs. Add sufficient water to mix to a stiff dough. On a lightly floured board roll out dough to a rectangle 0.5 to 1 cm thick. With the short end of the rectangle facing, dot two-thirds of the pastry with a third of the remaining butter to within 1 cm of the dough edge. Fold the one-third of pastry without any butter on it to the middle of the pastry. Fold the buttered section over the folded edge. Seal the edges with a rolling pin and mark the dough with the rolling pin to form corrugations. Give the pastry a quarter turn. Roll into a rectangle. Repeat the folding and rolling processes twice more until all the butter is used, chilling the pastry for 5 minutes between rollings if possible. Use as required for savoury pies and vol au vents. Makes 500 g pastry.

SHORT PASTRY

2 cups Champion standard
    plain flour
1/4 teaspoon salt
125 g butter
cold water

Sift flour and salt together. Cut in the butter until it resembles fine breadcrumbs. Mix to a stiff dough with a little water. Roll out very lightly and do not handle more than is necessary. Use as required for sweet or savoury pies and tarts, and quiches. Makes 375 g pastry.

WHOLEMEAL PASTRY

Replace flour with Champion wholemeal flour and add 1 teaspoon Edmonds baking powder.

SWEET SHORTCRUST PASTRY

1 cup Champion standard
    plain flour
75 g butter
1/4 cup sugar
1 egg yolk
1 tablespoon water

Sift flour. Cut in butter until it resembles fine breadcrumbs. Stir in sugar. Add egg yolk and water. Mix to a stiff dough. Chill for 30 minutes before using. Use as required for sweet pies and tarts. Makes about 400 g pastry.

SPICE PASTRY

Add 1 tablespoon mixed spice to flour.

NUT PASTRY

Add 1/2 cup chopped walnuts before mixing to a stiff dough.

FRENCH DRESSING (VINAIGRETTE)

3/4 cup oil
1/4 cup DYC white or cider vinegar
    or lemon juice
1/4 teaspoon dry mustard
salt
black pepper
1 clove garlic, crushed
1 tablespoon chopped parsley,
    chives or fresh basil

Put all ingredients into a screw-top jar. Shake well to combine. Makes 1 cup.

MUSTARD DRESSING

Add 2 teaspoons wholeseed mustard.

WHITE SAUCE

2 tablespoons butter
2 tablespoons Champion standard
    plain flour
1 cup milk
salt
pepper

Melt butter in a small saucepan. Stir in flour and cook until frothy. Gradually add milk stirring constantly. Stir over a medium heat until sauce boils and thickens. Cook for a further 2 minutes. Season with salt and pepper to taste. Makes 1 cup.

CHEESE SAUCE

Remove pan from heat. Stir in 1/2 cup grated tasty cheese after cooking sauce.

CURRY SAUCE

Add 1 to 2 teaspoons curry powder when adding flour.

EGG SAUCE

Add chopped whites of 3 hard-boiled eggs to sauce. Garnish with sieved yolks and chopped parsley.

ONION SAUCE

Add 1 sliced onion to butter and cook until clear. Continue as above.

PARSLEY SAUCE

Remove pan from heat. Add 2 to 4 tablespoons chopped parsley.

TOMATO SAUCE

Omit milk and use 1/2 cup tomato puree and 1/2 cup water.

BECHAMEL SAUCE

Stud an onion with 6 cloves. Place onion and milk in a small saucepan and bring almost to the boil. Strain. In a separate pan melt butter and continue as above. Add heated milk.

GLOSSARY

Al dente: Used to describe cooked pasta that is firm to the bite.

Bain marie is a water bath. The dish of food to be cooked is placed in a larger dish and surrounded with hot water to come half to three-quarters of the way up the food dish. This provides a gentle, more even heat for mixtures that are sensitive to direct heat.

Bake blind: To place a piece of baking paper in an unbaked pastry case, fill with dried beans or rice, and bake. This enables the pastry to bake with a flat base. Baking blind beans or rice can be stored and re-used.

Baking paper has a special coating on it to prevent sticking. It saves greasing tins or baking trays. For cake or slice tins, line the base of the tin with baking paper. There is no need to grease the sides of the tin. Once the food is cooked run a knife around the edges of the tin, pressing the knife blade against the tin to prevent damaging the cake or slice. Cover baking trays with baking paper to save greasing when baking biscuits.

Baking powder is a mixture of cream of tartar and baking soda plus wheat fillers, which helps the baking powder to flow easily.

Baking soda is also known as bicarbonate of soda.

Baste: To spoon juices over foods being roasted to prevent drying and to give a glossy surface.

Blanch: To place fruit and vegetables in boiling water briefly, then remove to cold water to ease removing of skins or prepare for freezing.

Blend: To mix ingredients thoroughly to get an even consistency.

Boil: To cook at boiling point with large rolling bubbles forming.

Bouquet garni is a mixture of parsley, thyme and bay leaf which is tied together with cotton if fresh herbs are used, or enclosed in a muslin bag if dried herbs are used. Bouquet garni is used as a flavouring for stocks. It should be removed once the cooking is completed.

Braise: To gently fry in fat then cook slowly in very little moisture, covered.

Chicken – to test whether chicken is cooked, pierce it in the thickest part with a skewer, satay stick or sharp knife. If the juices run clear, the chicken is cooked. If the juices are pink, further cooking is necessary.

Chilli oil is oil flavoured with fresh chillies. It can be bought already flavoured or fresh chillies can be steeped in oil to flavour your own. Use any oil you prefer, depending on its end use.

Chocolate curls are easily made using a potato peeler and "peeling" a piece of chocolate. Well-formed curls will be made if the chocolate is slightly soft.

Clarified butter is butter from which milk solids have been removed. Can be used for frying as it heats to a high temperature without burning. Known also as frying butter or ghee.

Coconut through this cookbook means desiccated unless otherwise stated. Coconut can be toasted by heating it in a frying pan over a moderate heat. Shake the pan from time to time. Remove pan from heat when coconut just starts to colour.

Coconut cream or coconut milk is available canned or powdered, or can be made by mixing $1\frac{1}{4}$ cups of coconut with 300 ml of boiling water then straining through a sieve and reserving the liquid. This will give about 1 cup (250 ml) of coconut milk.

Cold smoked salmon has a translucent look and is smoked without heat.

Cool pastry fillings – cold fillings should be used in pastry shells to prevent pastry becoming soggy on the bottom.

Cornflour is made from maize and is a starch used to thicken products such as sauces and desserts, or it can be used in some baked products.

Cream: To beat softened butter or other fat with sugar until light, fluffy and creamy in colour.

Curry powder is a mixture of spices and you can combine different spices in different amounts to make your own blend. Some of the basic spices might include cumin, coriander, ginger, cloves, fenugreek, turmeric and cinnamon. Whole spices can be ground with a mortar and pestle or prepared ground spices can be used.

Cut in: Using a knife, pastry blender, food processor or clean finger tips to combine fat with flour to get a crumb-like consistency.

Eggs should be at room temperature when making sponges and other baked goods as this produces a cake with better volume. Egg whites for making meringues and pavlovas should always be at room temperature.

Fold: Combining a delicate mixture with a heavier one by using a metal spoon in a cutting action, cutting down through centre and bringing bottom mixture to top. Used for additions of whipped cream and beaten egg whites.

Filo pastry is tissue paper thin pastry traditionally used for strudels. It can be bought in packets from the chiller and once opened should be used within a week to ten days. When working with filo pastry (sometimes written as phyllo) place it under a damp teatowel to prevent it from drying out and becoming brittle and hard to manage.

Fresh and dried herbs – as a rule of thumb replace a measure of fresh herbs with half the quantity of dried herbs. Double a dried measure if replacing with fresh herbs.

Fresh ginger is root ginger. This is available from the fruit and vegetables section of the supermarket and should be stored in the refrigerator crisper or frozen for easy grating. The ginger root can be peeled before using if wished.

Frothy: When making white sauce, heat butter and flour until mixture appears frothy with small bubbles before adding liquid.

Hot smoked salmon has the look of cooked fish and has been smoked with heat.

Jelly bag: A muslin or fine cloth bag that can be hung to allow jelly to drain through when preserving. A piece of muslin can be used by attaching it to the legs of an upturned chair before the jelly is drained through.

Knead: To press non-yeast doughs together to get an even texture. Yeast doughs are stretched and folded to develop elasticity. This is done by pushing the dough away from you with the heel of your hand then folding the dough over.

Lemons – Two main lemon types are grown in New Zealand, Meyer and Lisbon. Meyer lemons have a soft bright yellow flesh and semi-sweet flavour. They make a good garnish but do not have a lot of flavour in cooking. Lisbon lemons have a light, hard skin, a light lemon flesh and a sharper lemon taste. They should always be used in cooking where setting is required, as in condensed milk cheesecakes, lemon honey and lemon meringue pies.

Margarine can replace butter, giving a similar result. Extra flour may need to be added in some baked recipes to give the required consistency.

Marinate: To leave meat, poultry or fish in a tenderising or flavouring liquid (the marinade) for a period of time.

Mash: Food is crushed until soft. This can be done with a fork or a potato masher.

Measuring – all recipes have been developed using standard metric measuring cups and spoons. All measurements are level. For easiest measuring use measuring cups or jugs for liquid measures and sets of 1 cup, 1/2 cup and 1/4 cup for dry ingredients. Brown sugar measures are firmly packed so that the sugar will hold the shape of the cup when tipped out.

Nuts can be toasted in the oven or in a pan on top of the stove. To toast nuts in the oven, place in an oven dish and cook at 180°C for 5 to 15 minutes depending on the nuts. To toast on top of the stove, place nuts in a frying pan and cook over a moderate heat until just starting to colour. Toss nuts during cooking to prevent burning.

Olive oil is available in a variety of types. Light olive oil has the least flavour with the deeper green virgin olive oils having a distinct flavour. Use olive oil to make French dressing or vinaigrette. If using olive oil in cooking, take care not to overheat it as it will smoke at a lower temperature than many oils.

Pot measure refers to the size of the whole pot. When a 250 g pot measure is given it means use the whole pot.

Prepared mustard is wet mustard that has already been made or bought. Wholeseed or smooth varieties are available.

Purée: Cooked fruit or vegetables mashed or sieved to give a smooth semi-liquid product.

Roasted peppers – cut peppers in half lengthwise. Remove core and place cut side down on a baking tray. Bake at 200°C for 15 minutes or until skins are blistered and browned. When peppers are cool enough to handle remove skin. The skins on red and yellow peppers will blister and come away more easily than green peppers.

Rub in: To mix fat into flour by rubbing with fingers to get a crumb-like mixture.

Sambal oelak is a paste made from hot chillies and salt.

Sauté: To fry food in a small amount of hot fat quickly and with shaking or stirring of pan to get even cooking.

Scald – liquids are brought to boiling point.

Setting test for jam: Jam has reached its setting point and is ready for bottling when a small amount is placed on a cold saucer, left to cool, and will hold a channel when a finger is dragged through it.

Shallots are small brown-skinned onions similar in shape to a chestnut or large, slightly flat garlic clove. They have a mild onion flavour and are good for use in salads, dressings and casseroles or anything that requires a milder onion flavour.

Shards are long pointed pieces that look like broken glass. Praline is often broken into shards for impressive decoration.

Sieve: To pass through a mesh to get an even consistency.

Sift: To pass dry ingredients through a mesh to remove lumps, foreign matter or to mix evenly.

Simmer: To cook just at boiling point, not a full rolling boil.

Skim: To remove fat or scum from the surface of a liquid with a slotted spoon, spoon or absorbent paper.

Soft breadcrumbs are made from stale bread. They are not toasted.

Softened butter makes creaming butter and sugar easy. Butter can be softened in the microwave, left to stand in a warm place or softened over hot water. Softened butter is not the same as melted butter.

Spoons: A wooden spoon is used for stirring a heated mixture, as it does not become too hot to handle. It does not discolour pale mixtures as a metal one can do by scraping against the metal of the saucepan. Metal spoons, solid or slotted, are used for transferring foods; slotted ones will allow liquids to drain from solids.

Slotted spoons are useful for folding mixtures together. A metal spoon is best for folding or creaming butter and sugar by hand.

Steep: To leave food or flavouring to stand in liquid to absorb flavours.

Stiffly beaten egg white: Beaten until peaks formed will hold their shape, but tips bend over. Mixture should be glossy.

Stir-fry: To stir and toss prepared ingredients in hot oil very quickly, resulting in moist meats and crisp vegetables.

Stock can be homemade or bought in cartons as a liquid, in pots as a powder or as foil-wrapped cubes. One stock cube is the equivalent of 1 teaspoon of stock powder.

Tahini is a paste made from toasted sesame seeds and is widely used in Middle Eastern cooking. It has a toasted nut flavour.

Tepid – this is blood temperature, ie 37°C, and liquid feels neither hot nor cold when a drop is placed on the back of your hand.

Thick and glossy – when making meringue, egg whites and sugar are beaten until very stiff. This is when peaks stand up when the beaters are removed and the meringue should look shiny. An electric mixer should be used for this as it takes time and is too arduous to do by hand successfully. The sugar should be dissolved in the egg whites. Test by rubbing a little mixture between your fingers.

To cover steamed puddings: Tear a sheet of foil about 5 cm larger than the top of the basin. Make a pleat right across the sheet of foil. Cover basin with foil. Tie string very tightly around pudding basin just under the lip. Take a separate piece of string about 40 cm in length and fold in half. Secure the string at opposite ends of the basin to make a handle. This helps to get the pudding basin in and out of the saucepan.

Tomato paste is concentrated tomato purée.

Tomato purée is available in cans or can be made from fresh tomatoes in a blender or food processor.

Unmoulding jellies – a vacuum forms in the bottom of a jelly mould and this needs to be broken to release the jelly. Dip the mould in a bowl of hot water three times. Press the jelly around the edge, pulling it away gently with your finger. Turn mould onto a plate and shake sharply as you hold the plate and mould.

Yeast is used to raise bread, etc. 1 tablespoon of Edmonds active yeast equals 2 tablespoons of Edmonds Surebake active yeast mixture. And 1½ tablespoons dried yeast (1 sachet) equals 1 ounce or one cake of compressed yeast.

INDEX

BREADS & BUNS
Bagels 13
Chelsea Buns 13
Corn Bread..14
Focaccia Bread 17
Hot Cross Buns 14
Stollen 17

MUFFINS, LOAVES, SCONES
Blueberry Muffins 19
Bran Muffins 19
Corn, Cheese and Bacon Muffins...................20
Date Loaf (and Apricot variation) 20
Ginger Gems 21
Pikelets..23
Scones (Cheese, Date and Sultana variations) 23

CAKES
Banana Cake 25
Boiled Fruit Cake 25
Butter Cake (Lemon Syrup cake variation) 25
Cappuccino Cake 26
Carrot Cake 27
Cherry Almond Cake 27
Chocolate Éclairs (Cream Puffs variation) 28
Chocolate Log 29
Christmas Cake 30
Christmas Mince Pies.......................................30
Christmas Mincemeat 30
Cinnamon Cream Oysters or Fingers.............32
Continental Apple Cake 32
Eccles Cakes 33
Fielder's Sponge 35
Ginger Kisses 35
Gingerbread 36
Ladysmith Cake 36
Lamingtons 36
Light Fruit Cake with Toffee Nuts 38
Macaroon Cake 39
Madeira Cake 39
Mud Cake 40
One-Egg Chocolate Cake 40
Orange Cake 41
Semolina Cake 43
Simnel Cake 43
Sultana Cake 43
Tennis Cake 41

BISCUITS
Afghans 45
Almond Biscuits 45
Anzac Biscuits 45
Belgium Biscuits 46
Biscotti..47
Brandy Snaps 47
Duskies 48
Florentines 49
Hokey Pokey Biscuits.......................................49
Melting Moments...51
Meringues 51
Oat Biscuits 51
Peanut Brownies 52
Santé Biscuits 52
Shortbread 53
Yoyos 53

SLICES
Apple Shortcake Squares 55
Caramel Meringue 55
Caramel Slice 56
Chinese Chews 56
Chocolate Brownie 57
Coconut Dream 58
Date Shortcake 58
Fruit Squares 59
Ginger Crunch 60
Lemon Slice 60
Louise Cake 60
Marshmallow Shortcake 63
Peanut Shortcake 63

NIBBLES
Antipasto 67
Bacon-Wrapped Bananas 68
Chicken Liver Paté 71
Crostini 67
Devils on Horseback 68
Guacamole (Avocado Dip) 67
Hummus (Chick Pea Dip) 68
Onion Marmalade 71
Tomato Salsa 71

BREAKFASTS
Bacon Rashers 73
Bananas with Maple Syrup 73
Breakfast Mushrooms 73
Eggs Benedict 74
French Toast 74
Scrambled Egg (with variations).....................75
Toasted Muesli 75

LIGHT MEALS
Bacon and Egg Pie 77
Bacon and Tomato Risotto 81
French Onion Soup 78
Frittata 77
Hash Brown Potatoes 77
Pumpkin Soup 78
Quiche Lorraine 81
Rajah's Pizza (BLT variation) 83
Seafood Soup 79
Spicy Lentil Soup 79
Spinach and Smoked Salmon Roulade 83
Tuscan Tomato Soup 80

PASTA
Bolognese Sauce..87
Carbonara (Ham and Mushroom Sauce) 87
Fresh Tomato and Basil Sauce 88
Lasagne 88
Marinara (Seafood Sauce) 90
Pesto (Basil and Garlic Sauce) 91
Roasted Pepper and Pumpkin Lasagne........91
Smoked Salmon Pasta Sauce 93
Spinach and Bacon Sauce...............................93

SEAFOOD
Baked Lemon and Sage Fish........................105
Crispy Chinese Batter.....................................95
Fish Pie..95
Italian Baked Fish 96

Mussel Soup 97
Poisson Cru 101
Salmon Steaks (with Thai Dipping Sauce) 98
Scallops Mornay 101
Seafood Cocktail 105
Sir Walter's Oysters 97
Smoked Salmon Hash Browns 101
Spanish Paella 98
Squid Rings 102
Stir Fried Lemon and Ginger Fish 95
Thai Fish Cakes 103
Whitebait Fritters 105

MEAT
Beef Olives (Pork Olives variation) 107
Beef Stroganoff..107
Beef or Lamb Satays with Peanut Sauce 108
Boeuf Bourguignon 108
Chilli and Coriander Marinated Steak 109
Corned Beef 109
Ginger Beef Stir-Fry 110
Indian Beef Curry..110
Lamb Racks with Redcurrant Sauce 111
Lamb Shanks in Red Wine 113
Roast Lamb with Fresh Mint Chutney 113
Shepherd's Pie 114
Sweet and Sour Pork 114
Veal Cordon Bleu (Chicken Cordon Bleu variation) 115

CHICKEN
Chicken and Apricot Filo Parcels 117
Chicken and Avocado Salad 117
Chicken and Pesto Bake 117
Chicken Paprika 118
Chicken Pie 118
Chicken Stir-Fry with Cashews 119
Coq-au-Vin 121
Marinated Chicken Wings 121
Roast Stuffed Chicken (with Sausagemeat, Orange
 & Rosemary and Apricot stuffing variations) 122
Thai Chicken Curry 122

VEGETABLES
Caesar Salad..125
Greek Salad 125
Grilled Vegetables with Vinaigrette 126
Ratatouille 126
Spinach Salad 129
Sweetcorn Fritters 129
Tuscan Potatoes with Sundried Tomatoes 129

COLD DESSERTS
Baked Lemon Cheesecake 133
Cassata..133
Chilled Cheesecake......................................134
Crème Caramel 135
Easy Chocolate Mousse
 (Chocolate Liqueur Mousse variation) 135
Flourless Chocolate Cake 137
Fruit Flan 137
Iced Coffee 138
Lemon Tart 138
Lemon Yoghurt Ice Cream Terrine 138
Orange-Marinated Strawberries 140
Pavlova 141

Plum and Port Jelly 140
Sherry Trifle 142
Sorbet..142
Summer Berries with Praline and Custard 144
Summer Pudding 144
Tiramisù 145

HOT PUDDINGS
Apple Pie 147
Apple Strudel 147
Bread and Butter Pudding 148
Chocolate Self-Saucing Pudding 148
Christmas Pudding......................................151
Crème Brûlée 151
Fruit Crumble (with Wholemeal and Wholegrain
 Oat Crumble and Fruit Betty variations) 152
Lemon Meringue Pie 152
Pear Tarte Tatin 154
Pecan Pie 155
Sticky Date Pudding with Caramel Sauce........155

PRESERVES
Apricot Jam 159
Fetta and Olive Preserve..............................159
Indian Mango Chutney 159
Kiwifruit Relish 164
Lemon Honey 160
Marmalade..160
Pickled Onions 160
Pickled Vegetables 162
Plum Jam 163
Plum Sauce 163
Preserved Lemons..163
Raspberry Jam (with Boysenberry variation) 164
Strawberry Jam 164
Sweet Pickled Gherkins 167
Tomato Sauce..167

ICINGS, CUSTARD, PASTRIES,
DRESSINGS & SAUCES
Bechamel Sauce 169
Butter Icing 168
Cheese Sauce 169
Chocolate Icing 168
Coffee Icing 168
Cream Cheese Icing 168
Curry Sauce 169
Edmonds Custard..168
Egg Sauce 169
Flaky Pastry 168
French Dressing (Vinaigrette) 169
White Icing 168
Lemon Icing 168
Mustard Dressing 169
Nut Pastry 169
Onion Sauce..169
Orange Icing 168
Parsley Sauce 169
Pink Icing 168
Short Pastry 169
Spice Pastry 169
Sweet Shortcrust Pastry 169
Tomato Sauce..169
Wholemeal Pastry 169
White Sauce..169

ACKNOWLEDGEMENTS

Some china supplied by Studio of Tableware, Mt Eden.

ISBN 1-86958-625-5

© 1998 Text and Photography Bluebird Foods Ltd

First published in 1998 by Hodder Moa Beckett Publishers Limited
Reprinted in 1998, Second reprint 1998

Published by Hodder Moa Beckett Publishers Limited
[a member of the Hodder Headline Group]
4 Whetu Place, Mairangi Bay, Auckland, New Zealand

Art Directed, Designed, Produced and Typeset by Hodder Moa Beckett Publishers Ltd

Text and Food Styling by Robyn Martin
Photography by Alan Gilliard
Scanning and Film produced by Microdot
Printed by Toppan Printing Co Ltd. Singapore

All rights reserved. No part of this publication may be reproduced or transmitted in any form or by any means, electronic or mechanical, including photocopying, recording, or any information storage and retrieval system, without permission in writing from the publisher.